Clear Speech

From the Start

Basic Pronunciation and
Listening Comprehension
in North American English

2ⁿᵈ Edition

Teacher's Resource and Assessment Book

Judy B. Gilbert

CAMBRIDGE
UNIVERSITY PRESS

CAMBRIDGE
UNIVERSITY PRESS

32 Avenue of the Americas, New York, NY 10013-2473, USA

Cambridge University Press is part of the University of Cambridge.

It furthers the University's mission by disseminating knowledge in the pursuit of education, learning and research at the highest international levels of excellence.

Distributed By:
Grass Roots Press
Toll Free: 1-888-303-3213
Fax: (780) 413-6582
Web Site: www.grassrootsbooks.net

lge.org/9781107604315

First published 2001
3rd printing 2014

Printed in Hong Kong, China, by Golden Cup Printing Company Limited

A catalog record for this publication is available from the British Library.

ISBN 978-1-107-68715-8 Student's Book
ISBN 978-1-107-60431-5 Teacher's Resource and Assessment Book
ISBN 978-1-107-61172-6 Class and Assessment Audio CDs

For a full list of components, visit www.cambridge.org/clearspeech

Art direction, ████████████████████████ search: Q2A/Bill Smith
Audio produc████████████████████

"Lone Jack to Kno██ ████ by ███ Rummel from his █, Lone Jack: The Ragtime of Today

Apple, iPad, iPho███ ████████████████ are trademarks of Apple Inc., registered in the U.S. and other countries. App Store is a service mark of Apple Inc., registered in the U.S. and other countries.

Contents

Appendices

Extra Practice 1 – Vowels

Extra Practice 2 – Problem Consonants

Tests and Quizzes

Letter to the Teacher

From the first edition, *Clear Speech From the Start* has concentrated on the way that musical signals of spoken English are used to show emphasis – that is, stress, vowel lengthening, and pitch change. If the emphasis signals are clear, English listeners will understand the message even if there are errors in individual sounds. Conversely, even if the sounds are fairly clear, errors in emphasis or stress might confuse the listener.

Now this second edition of *Clear Speech From the Start*, revised with valuable feedback from teachers, adds new support to help you teach your students these musical signals of spoken English. This letter outlines the new features of both the Student's Book and this Teacher's Resource and Assessment Book.

New Features of *Clear Speech From the Start*, Second Edition

A pronunciation pyramid adds new support.

This concept makes it easier for students to understand how the various aspects of spoken English work together.

The pyramid is divided into four levels, each with a distinctive color. (You will find the full-color pyramid on page x of the Student's Book.) The base, or foundation, level of the pyramid is the *word group* (or *thought group*, a short sentence, a clause, or a phrase). Within that base, there is a *most important word* (or *focus word*). This word is the focus of meaning in each word group. Within the most important word, there is one *strong syllable* (or most *stressed syllable*). The vowel at the center of this syllable is the *peak vowel*, which is the top of the pyramid and the peak of information. Accuracy is necessary when pronouncing this vowel.

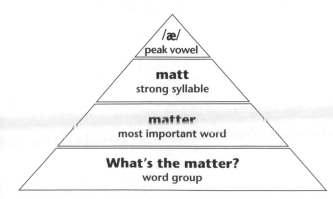

Throughout the Student's Book, the pyramid appears at appropriate points to remind students how the specific topic being taught fits into the whole system of spoken English. With the same purpose, Rules and Vowel Work boxes are shaded in the pyramid level color that corresponds to the topic being presented.

More support for vowel rules is given.

Sound symbols are used in specific tasks to help students recognize that the sound may be different than the letter, and how pronunciation of sounds relates to the spelling rules. A chart with the percentage of time these rules actually work is given on pages 132–133 of the Student's Book.

Expanded appendices provide extra practice of problem consonants.

In addition to the revised extra practice of vowel and vowel rules, the appendices in the back of the Student's Book now present and practice some common problem consonants.

A color design adds visual appeal and clarity to presentation and practice.

A color design as well as updated illustrations and graphics make the presentations even clearer and provide more support for the practice tasks.

The audio program is available for students to download.

The complete audio program for the listening tasks in the Student's Book is available as MP3s on the website www.cambridge.org/clearspeech. Students can now download the audio for further practice outside the classroom.

An app with games makes self-study practice more engaging.

Four games with hundreds of activities provide further practice of key pronunciation aspects. The *Basic Pronunciation: Clear Speech From the Start* App for iPhone, iPad, and iPod touch is available on the App Store.

Features of the Teacher's Resource and Assessment Book

This Teacher's Resource and Assessment Book includes the following features, all of which enhance the teaching of the Student's Book and help teachers manage their pronunciation lessons more effectively.

Unit overviews

Each unit begins with a description of its main teaching points, to facilitate class planning.

Task descriptions

These task descriptions include a variety of presentation ideas as well as useful theoretical background information. Tasks marked in the Teacher's Resource and Assessment Book by the headphones icon 🎧 are included on the Class Audio CDs. The CD and track numbers are also provided to help teachers quickly access the material on the Class Audio program.

Audio scripts

All of the material on the Class Audio program that does not appear on the pages of the Student's Book is presented in the audio scripts. Scripts for the "Which word do you hear?" and "Which word is different?" tasks contain phonetic transcriptions. Teachers can use the transcriptions as a pronunciation guideline when reading the items themselves or to help clarify the pronunciation of specific items for students. A key to the phonetic symbols used in the Teacher's Resource and Assessment Book can be found on pages xiv–xv.

Answer keys

All of the answers to tasks that require students to come up with specific responses are included. Suggested answers are also given for some of the open-ended tasks. These should help guide students that might have trouble coming up with their own answers for such tasks.

Teaching tips

These are expansion activities or further presentation ideas that reinforce or extend the points students are learning in the unit. They can add more fun and variety to the lessons.

Clear Listening Diagnostic Test and Clear Speaking Diagnostic Test

Both of these photocopiable tests can be used either at the beginning of the course to determine which areas students need improvement or at the end of the course to provide students with a measure of their progress. The audio for the listening test is available on the Assessment Audio CD packed with the Class Audio CDs.

Pronunciation Profile Form

This photocopiable form can be used to evaluate students' performance in the Clear Speaking Diagnostic Test.

Unit quizzes

Photocopiable quizzes are provided for Units 1 through 15. The quizzes are designed to be given after the completion of each unit, and they have been revised and expanded for the second edition. The audio for the quizzes is available on the Assessment Audio CD.

Test and quizzes audio scripts and answer keys

This section includes the audio scripts and answer keys for all the tasks in the listening test and unit quizzes. It also indicates the Assessment Audio CD track number for the recording for each task. Directions for reading the test and quizzes tasks out loud for the students are also provided.

Glossary

The glossary defines terms used in the Student's Book in nontechnical language that is suitable for student comprehension.

Bibliography

The bibliography provides reference to information cited in the Teacher's Resource and Assessment Book or provides further reading for a teacher's own research.

Components of *Clear Speech From the Start*, Second Edition

Student's Book

The Student's Book makes understanding the key concepts of English pronunciation easier with simple and clear explanations, aided by a variety of oral, visual, and kinesthetic resources. Practical rules and a variety of practice activities help students improve their listening and speaking skills. Appendices at the end of the book provide useful reference material and extra practice for more advanced classes.

Teacher's Resource and Assessment Book

This book provides practical explanations for the rationale for each lesson, useful classroom procedures, teaching tips, as well as the audio script and answer key for each task. It also includes a listening diagnostic test, a speaking diagnostic test and a student's pronunciation profile form, 15 unit quizzes, and all the audio scripts and answer keys.

Class Audio and Assessment Audio CDs

This set includes three Class Audio CDs with the audio for all the listening tasks in the Student's Book and one Assessment Audio CD with the audio for all the tasks in the listening test and unit quizzes.

App

The App *Basic Pronunciation*: *Clear Speech From the Start* for iPhone, iPad, and iPod touch includes hundreds of fun interactive activities for engaging practice with word stress, syllables, and beginning and final sounds. It is available on the App Store.

Website

The website www.cambridge.org/clearspeech provides extra materials and information about the series, including the complete audio for all the listening activities in the Student's Book as downloadable MP3s.

I hope that you find using this second edition of *Clear Speech From the Start* to be an enjoyable and professionally rewarding experience.

Judy B. Gilbert

Introduction

This introduction explains the approach to pronunciation reflected in *Clear Speech From the Start*, Second Edition. It will help you understand why the book is organized as it is and why it emphasizes the "musical" aspects of English: rhythm, stress, and intonation. This introduction also presents some pedagogical reflections and recommendations that can help you make the most of your pronunciation lessons.

Linguistic underpinnings

Here is a sad story: A teacher has just completed a successful pronunciation lesson using minimal pairs of words to teach the sounds /r/ and /l/. All of the students were able to manage the distinction by the end of the lesson. The students feel good and the teacher feels good. Then, as the students are leaving the room, one student turns to the teacher and cheerfully says, "So rong!" The teacher does not feel so good anymore.

The fact is that minimal pair practice alone sometimes yields minimal results. This may be part of the reason that the teaching of pronunciation has fallen into disfavor in so many programs. Lack of success is discouraging to teachers, and students sometimes feel that pronunciation is an endless succession of unrelated and unmanageable pieces. If the work is so discouraging, shouldn't we just drop it? Why should we include pronunciation in the curriculum?

There are two fundamental reasons to teach pronunciation. First of all, students need to understand, and, secondly, they need to be understood. If they are not able to understand spoken English well, or if they cannot be understood easily, they are cut off from the language, except in its written form.

The relationship between speaking and listening comprehension

Intelligibility involves both speaking and listening comprehension. Following are two commonplace situations that, taken together, illustrate this fact. In the first situation, say in a bus station in an English-speaking country, a low-level student eagerly tries out something that has been carefully rehearsed in class, only to find out that the other person does not understand and even breaks off the interaction with a show of irritation. Native speakers are not necessarily unpleasant by nature, but they are often in a hurry and, unlike ESL/EFL teachers, they are not professionally patient. A few humiliating experiences like this one may make learners so discouraged that they give up trying. Such a student may continue to attend classes, but may also stop believing that there is much use in making an effort. And as you know, discouraged students are hard to teach.

Here is another situation, this time set in the workplace: A new employee, who is not a native speaker of English, is approached by a supervisor, who is a native speaker. The supervisor says something that sounds like, "It's very important to *schussel* the *wozzick*." The employee, not really understanding but eager to make a good impression, nods enthusiastically and says, "Important, yes, yes!" Later, the supervisor returns to find the task not done, or done incorrectly. What conclusion is apt to be reached? That the worker is dishonest? Stupid? Lazy? Unfortunately, few supervisors would realize that the problem came from inadequate listening comprehension. That is why English instruction must address the relationship between pronunciation and listening comprehension. This is true for students at every level, regardless of their proficiency in writing and reading English.

The relationship between rhythm and reading

Not known to many teachers, there is a bonus benefit to practicing speaking with English rhythm: a useful effect on learning to read in English. The reason for the effect is that rhythm affects the way people hear sounds. If the timing is wrong, it's hard to identify the sound accurately. Since people from other languages tend to hear and speak in the rhythm / timing of their first language, this can affect the clarity of their listening perception. And if you can't efficiently catch the clarity of sounds that make up words, research shows that it slows down your ability to tie sounds to letters in reading. For this reason, getting the new rhythm right can actually help students identify the sequence of sounds, a precondition to literacy in the target language that reading specialists refer to as *phonological awareness*. (David et al., 2007; Wade-Wooley & Wood, 2006; Wood, 2006; Goswami & Bryant, 1990).

Segmentals and suprasegmentals

There are two main components of pronunciation: the *segmentals* and the *suprasegmentals*. The word "segmentals" refers to individual sounds. For instance, look at the first lines of this song, a Canadian version of a popular U.S. folk song:

This land is your land,
This land is my land,
From Bonavista to Vancouver Island.

If the sounds represented by the letters -l-, -b-, and -v- in these lines are not said correctly, intelligibility will be harmed. But suprasegmentals also affect intelligibility. The word "suprasegmentals" refers to the musical qualities of rhythm, stress, and intonation that carry the sounds along and help convey emphasis and coherence. For instance, in this song, it is important that extra length be given to the word "your" in the first line and "my" in the next line because this emphasis links the two words together to mean "yours and mine together." In English, suprasegmentals are mainly used to signal emphasis and the relationship between ideas.

Why are the musical signals (suprasegmentals) of a new language so important?

Following are two sentences that are almost identical.

a. We have a lot of money.
b. We had a lot of money.

The only difference between these sentences is a contrast of *segmentals*. That is, the final consonant sounds in "have" and "had." Is this difference important? Yes, of course. But the other component, the suprasegmentals, must be considered as well. Consider, for example, how different emphasis patterns might change the meaning of each sentence.

Now consider the following sentences, which are also almost identical.

a. John said, "The boss is late!"
b. "John," said the boss, "is late!"

Who was speaking in each sentence? When reading the sentences, the written punctuation marks let us know who was speaking. In the spoken form, however, there are no visible punctuation marks. Furthermore, practice distinguishing the individual sounds in each sentence would not help a learner understand the difference in meaning.

Students may have learned to understand written punctuation, but they also need to be alert to signals that group words. These signals are in the music of the language and are significant both for intelligibility and for effective listening. This book practices these signals mainly in grouping numbers, as in a telephone number. If the numbers aren't grouped in the way people are used to hearing them, they will be harder to understand.

One American teaching trainee had this to say at the end of a pronunciation methods course:

When I began the class, I expected to learn techniques for teaching the individual sounds, but now I believe pronunciation is bigger than that. Now I think trying to teach somebody pronunciation without paying attention to the suprasegmentals is like teaching somebody ballroom dancing, only without music, without a partner, and standing still.

On reading this comment, a Japanese teacher in the class said, "You could also say that trying to learn English pronunciation without suprasegmentals is like trying to learn swimming on a *tatami* (straw mat) floor."

Alexander Graham Bell, who was deeply concerned with both hearing and intelligibility, wrote:

Ordinary people who know nothing of phonetics or elocution have difficulties in understanding slow speech composed of perfect sounds, while they have no difficulty in comprehending an imperfect gabble if only the accent and rhythm are natural. (Bell, 1916)

In other words, when the suprasegmentals (musical signals) are right, the individual sound errors are more or less unimportant. That is, the listener pays more attention to the emphasis than to the individual sounds. I would also add that the individual sounds have a better chance of being pronounced accurately if they are said with the right timing.

English uses suprasegmentals to help the listener follow the thoughts of the speaker – to know which words are important and how they are connected. Other languages tend to use other means to indicate which words are important and to show how ideas are related, but spoken English relies mainly on the suprasegmental cues of rhythm, stress, and intonation – the "music" of the spoken language.

Rhythm

Children learn the rhythm of their first language in the first months of life. By the age of six months to a year, they are deeply familiar with that rhythm and thereafter unconsciously apply it to any new language they learn. It is therefore strategically important to bring the system of English rhythm to students' conscious attention.

The topic of rhythm is introduced in Unit 3 of the Student's Book, where students learn about the basic unit of English rhythm: the syllable. The topic is thereafter spiraled throughout the remaining units, and English rhythm is practiced through many activity types designed to fit a variety of learning styles.

Stress patterns (strong syllables)

Misplaced stress is one of the major sources of conversation breakdown. In fact, stress is so significant for intelligibility that English speakers systematically use several simultaneous signals of stress. The most crucial of these signals are *vowel lengthening* and *contrastive clarity*. English learners must be given ample opportunity to use the signals automatically, but these signals are best addressed one at a time. Units 5 and 6 of the Student's Book provide practice with recognizing and using these signals. They also provide two simple rules for stress. Consolidation of stress cues will prepare students to learn about one of the most important topics in *Clear Speech From the Start*: emphasizing the most important word (*intonational emphasis*).

Intonational emphasis (the most important word)

Each English *word group* (a short sentence, clause, or phrase) has one *most-important word* (the *focus word*). This is the word that the speaker wants the listener to notice most. All languages have a way to call attention to the most important idea in a group of words, but unlike many languages, English depends mainly on intonation to help the listener notice the focus word. That is, by changing the pitch on the *strong* (*stressed*) *syllable* of a focus word, the speaker gives emphasis to that word and, thereby, highlights it for the listener. Because other languages use other means to call attention to the important idea, learners tend not to notice this specifically English system for signaling emphasis.

Units 5 and 6 are meant to develop the ability to stress some syllables while obscuring others. This contrast between strong/stressed and reduced/weak syllables is essential to drawing strong attention to the most important word in a given word group. Unit 7 is about this most important word, the focus of meaning in the word group.

For the sake of simplicity and learnability, the Student's Book discusses emphasis within the context of a sentence. That is, students learn that a sentence has one or more most important words, and they learn to identify and emphasize those words.

Segmentals (vowels and consonants)

Although *Clear Speech From the Start* concentrates on the music of the spoken language (rhythm, stress, and intonation), the Student's Book also gives a great deal of attention to individual sounds, both vowels and consonants. Students need to hear these sounds many times in order to be able to develop awareness of the boundaries which define the sounds; for example, the distinction between /æ/ as in "man," and /ɛ/ as in "men." When they have a clear acoustic image of the differences, they have an accurate mental inventory of English sounds to rely on when both speaking and listening.

Vowel sounds are presented early in the Student's Book (Units 1 and 4) in order to prepare students for work with word stress (strong syllables). Since words are stressed by adding length and clarity to the vowel in a particular syllable, it is important for students to have good control of a basic set of English vowels if they are to practice English stress patterns. More information on the vowel rules are provided in Appendices B and C and more practice of these is available in Extra Practice 1 in the back of the Student's Book.

Units 8 through 15 deal with topics related to consonant sounds. Useful diagrams for some of the consonants focused in this book can be found in Appendix D and some common problem consonants are focused on and practiced in Extra Practice 2 in the back of the book.

Once students have learned about the musical aspects of English, they will be prepared to practice the individual consonants more efficiently. The target sounds are easier to produce and hear accurately when they are practiced in words and sentences with correct rhythm, stress, and intonation.

For more detailed information on the layout of the Student's Book, refer to the Scope and Sequence on pages vi–vii of that book, which highlights all of the major topics covered.

Pedagogical reflections

These are ideas I have collected over many years of teaching and talking to other pronunciation teachers. I hope that you find them useful.

The spoken language is different from the written language.

Most students assume that the written language and spoken language are identical. But in fact, there are many differences between written and spoken English. A vocabulary item is not really possessed until it is understood both in its printed form and in terms of its stress-affected spoken form.

Learning a second language is different from learning a first language.

Children learn to recognize the sounds and music of their first language within their first year of life. As part of that early learning process, they also learn to ignore the sounds and musical patterns that are not part of their mother tongue. In other words, they learn what to listen for and what not to listen for. For this reason, learning a second language involves not only becoming familiar with new sounds and melodies, but it also involves learning the ability to temporarily set aside sounds and patterns required for clarity in the first language. Some people seem to have an intuitive gift that allows them to pay attention to the sounds and music of a new language, but most students need to have these elements consciously brought to their attention since their first language is so deeply rooted in their psyche.

Pronunciation is very personal.

Good pronunciation in a new language requires a student, in a sense, to adopt a new persona. Some people find this easy to do, but most people do not. Many students tend to feel threatened by the idea of adopting the sounds and music of a new language. This is because the new sounds and different rhythm cause them to sound foreign to themselves. Typically, this reaction is not consciously recognized by the learner, but it is nonetheless a true barrier to adaptation. Teachers need to recognize that while grammar and vocabulary are difficult to learn, they do not present the same psychological difficulties for students as pronunciation. This is because the sounds and music of one's first language are learned so early that they are part of who we are and what group we belong to.

In some cases, students' discomfort with learning new pronunciation patterns may be so strong as to cause students to resist. Generally, this resistance manifests itself in a student not really absorbing what is being taught, or perhaps showing impatience or boredom. If the teacher or the other students get impatient with the uneasy learner, progress inevitably becomes even more difficult. In fact, even kindly teachers can intimidate a threatened student simply by their eagerness to help, especially when that eagerness results in teaching too many points at a pace faster than the concepts can be absorbed.

In this Teacher's Resource and Assessment Book, I suggest several ways that teachers can reduce the effect of these psychological obstacles to learning English pronunciation.

Adults can improve their pronunciation.

Adults may not be as malleable as young people, and so their habitual speech may not change much. However, that does not mean they cannot benefit from knowing how to fix a breakdown in communication if lack of intelligibility causes trouble in a particular situation.

"Accent addition" is better than "accent reduction."

The psychological difference between these two expressions is that instead of concentrating on erasing an accent, it is better to think about helping students add a different way of saying something when they have a practical reason to communicate with native speakers

Conscientious teachers often ask, "How can we reduce student errors?" It is useful to turn that question around and ask, "How can we increase student clarity?" Instead of trying to remove mispronunciation, which is often simply a transfer of something from the first language, it is more helpful for teachers to concentrate on adding new elements required by the target language.

The workload should be limited to what actually can be achieved.

If a task seems to be extra difficult, consider putting it off until the class has been refreshed by an activity they can complete successfully. This can help build a rising momentum of confidence, and a confident student is better able to learn.

Time is short, so priority topics are enough for now.

Teachers naturally want their students to achieve great clarity of speech in a relatively short time. There are two problems with this natural tendency:

a. Pronunciation improvement tends to be slow and not regular.

b. An overloaded student tends not to learn anything well.

For these reasons, it is better to restrict the topics to be mastered to those elements that are most important for intelligibility and listening comprehension. Each element should be practiced through different types of tasks until it is solidly learned. Later, when students have a solid foundation in these elements, they can be taught more subtle aspects of pronunciation.

Nervousness has a negative effect on pronunciation.

Nervousness tends to develop when students feel they are slipping behind others or when they feel that they are under too much pressure to perform well. Such nervousness has an especially negative effect on pronunciation. It is generally hard, for instance, for students to be courageous when called on to recite words or phrases alone. For this reason, it is preferable to have students recite words and phrases in chorus with the rest of the class (see the section on Quality Repetition below). Another way to lessen student tension is to use pair work. This type of activity requires students to pay attention only to their partners and protects them from feeling like the focus of class awareness.

Variety helps.

Students need a lot of practice to fix rhythm and other elements of pronunciation into their physical memory. However, extended drills can become boring, and boredom causes students' attention to wander. In order to get enough practice without getting the "vacant stare" effect, it is necessary to vary activities as much as possible, all the while continuing work on the same topic. For this reason, each unit in *Clear Speech From the Start* includes a variety of activity types. Following are descriptions of some of these activity types.

Listening tasks

Focused listening activities provide a solid foundation for confident, accurate speaking. The "Which word do you hear?" and "Which word is different?" tasks that appear throughout the Student's Book, for instance,

help students learn to recognize and distinguish between particular sounds and stress patterns. These tasks also prepare students for the speaking activities that follow.

Pair work

Pair work activities provide a communicative challenge and give students – even in very large classes – the opportunity to practice speaking and hearing English. These activities also provide the immediate feedback so important to motivation. Moreover, they place more responsibility for learning where it belongs – with the student.

Kinesthetic tasks

Having students move some part of their bodies (by raising a hand, a finger, or even just their eyebrows) or having them actually get up and move around the room, can help imprint a pronunciation element into students' physical memory. Put another way, kinesthetic work can help students physically internalize pronunciation elements such as rhythm and stress.

Music of English boxes

Learning the pronunciation of a second language is something like learning to play tennis. If you concentrate too much on trying to remember what to do with your wrist and, at the same time, try to remember how to position your feet, shoulders, and knees while also trying to remember to keep your eye on the ball, the combination of too many things to think about tends to keep you from putting everything together in a flowing movement. Although a tennis player needs to know all of these things, it works better if they can be learned holistically or impressionistically in order to get a clear mental image of what the flow of the stroke should feel like.

Similarly, when learning pronunciation, if a student is asked to think simultaneously about where to place the tongue, how to let the air flow, how to link words with preceding and following words, as well as what stress and intonation pattern to use, the complications become so great that the student cannot be expected to produce fluent, natural-sounding speech. A more productive approach is to help students form an acoustic impression of a short piece of language as a whole and learn it deeply, and only then to work toward understanding the specific elements that flow together to form it into English speech. This is the purpose of the Music of English tasks that appear throughout the Student's Book.

Pyramid reviews

Some units end with review tasks in which students are asked to fill in some of the levels of the pronunciation pyramid. These tasks can help students gradually practice noticing the key elements in a word group, especially how the most important word is emphasized through making its strong vowel the peak of information.

Quality Repetition helps students learn the rhythm, melody, and sounds of a new language.

Repetition is an old principle of language learning, but teachers quite naturally worry that many repetitions will lead to boredom. The fact is that boredom depends on how the repetition is done. Quality Repetition is based on a neurologically well-founded approach to learning the rhythm, melody, and sounds of language. Used primarily with Music of English activities, this approach depends both on highly varied encouragements to repeat a short chunk of language at fluent speed and on the psychological support of a choral setting. By repeating a short sentence or phrase in chorus, students learn the phrase "like a little song," fixing it in solid memory. Students reciting words or phrases alone tend to become uncertain and thus lose the rhythmic and melodic markers necessary to make the utterance clearly intelligible. Choral support, on the other hand, encourages each member of the group to stay exactly within the rhythmic structure.

The double purpose of this sort of practice is to give students personal possession of a fixed template of spoken English (which can later be used to analyze the core elements) and to provide a rising momentum of confidence for the class as a whole. This rising confidence outweighs any tendency to boredom because students are pleased to feel growing strength with each repetition.

> We are what we repeatedly do –
> Excellence is not an act but a habit.
>
> – Aristotle

Teaching and learning pronunciation can be rewarding experiences.

Many teachers think of pronunciation as a dauntingly technical subject, and they worry about looking professionally inadequate before their classes. This can lead them to teach in a way that emphasizes criticism, or it can lead them to try to teach too much, causing both teachers and students to lose confidence. The result is a common reluctance to teach pronunciation. In this Teacher's Resource and Assessment Book, I suggest several concepts and techniques to make the teaching of pronunciation a source of enjoyment and pride for both teacher and student.

Key to Sound Symbols

Vowels			
Key words	Clear Speech From the Start	Cambridge Dictionary of American English/ International Phonetic Alphabet	Your dictionary
cake, mail, pay	/eʸ/	/eɪ/	
pan, bat, hand	/æ/	/æ/	
tea, feet, key	/iʸ/	/iː/	
ten, well, red	/ɛ/	/e/	
ice, pie, night	/ɑʸ/	/ɑɪ/	
is, fish, will	/ɪ/	/ɪ/	
cone, road, know	/oʷ/	/oʊ/	
top, rock, stop	/ɑ/	/ɑ/	
blue, school, new, cube, few	/uʷ/	/uː/	
cut, cup, us, rust, love	/ʌ/	/ʌ/	
house, our, cow	/ɑʷ/	/ɑʊ/	
saw, talk, applause	/ɔ/	/ɔː/	
boy, coin, join	/ɔʸ/	/ɔɪ/	
put, book, woman	/ʊ/	/ʊ/	
alone, open, pencil, atom, ketchup	/ə/	/ə/	

Key words	Clear Speech From the Start	Cambridge Dictionary of American English/ International Phonetic Alphabet	Your dictionary
Consonants			
bid, jo**b**	/b/	/b/	
do, fee**d**	/d/	/d/	
food, sa**f**e, lea**f**	/f/	/f/	
go, do**g**	/g/	/g/	
home, be**h**ind	/h/	/h/	
kiss, ba**ck**	/k/	/k/	
load, poo**l**, fai**l**	/l/	/l/	
man, plu**m**	/m/	/m/	
need, ope**n**	/n/	/n/	
sa**ng**, si**n**k	/ŋ/	/ŋ/	
pen, ho**p**e	/p/	/p/	
road, ca**r**d	/r/	/r/	
see, re**c**ent	/s/	/s/	
show, na**t**ion, wa**sh**	/ʃ/	/ʃ/	
team, mea**t**	/t/	/t/	
choose, wa**tch**	/tʃ/	/tʃ/	
think, bo**th**, tee**th**	/θ/	/θ/	
this, fa**th**er, tee**th**e	/ð/	/ð/	
visit, sa**v**e, lea**v**e	/v/	/v/	
watch, a**w**ay	/w/	/w/	
yes, onion	/y/	/j/	
zoo, the**s**e, ea**s**e	/z/	/z/	
bei**g**e, mea**s**ure, A**s**ia	/ʒ/	/ʒ/	
jump, bri**dg**e	/dʒ/	/dʒ/	

1 The Alphabet and Vowels

Cake, please.

Unit overview

This unit introduces the letters of the alphabet, with special attention paid to the vowels. Students need immediate help figuring out how to pronounce written English, so that they can practice on their own what they have learned in class. English spelling is complicated and, unlike many other languages, the letter combinations are not always pronounced in the same way. The vowel letters are particularly challenging because each one represents at least two different sounds. Also, some of these sounds may not exist in the student's first language.

The traditional approach for teaching native English-speaking children how to read by "sounding out the letters" is not really suitable for students who do not know all the sounds of English yet (e.g., the /æ/ in "cat" or the /ɪ/ in "sit"). Furthermore, if they come from a non-alphabetic language, such as Mandarin or Thai, they did not learn the skill of hearing sounds in sequence. Therefore, this course takes a completely different approach, more appropriate to new-language learners.

∩ A The alphabet
Class CD 1, Track 2

Students will hear the name of each letter in the alphabet. This exercise is just for listening, so ask students not to pronounce the letter names yet. (That will begin in Unit 2.) Encouraging students to hold off on producing new sounds (or words) gives them a chance to develop a clear acoustic imprint of these sounds and avoids confusing them with their own attempts at production before they are ready.

∩ B Vowel letters
Class CD 1, Track 3

Students should just listen to the names of the vowel letters. They should not repeat them at this stage.

∩ C Do you hear a?
Class CD 1, Track 4

Tasks C through G help students learn to identify the *vowel sounds* that they hear, which is an important step before being asked to say them.

For your reference, see page xiv of this Teacher's Resource and Assessment Book for the Key to Sound Symbols.

Audio Script

1.	cake	/keᵏk/
2.	rice	/rɑᵏs/
3.	pay	/peᵏ/
4.	so	/soʷ/
5.	seat	/siᵏt/
6.	make	/meᵏk/

Answer Key

	Yes	No
1.	✓	
2.		✓
3.	✓	
4.		✓
5.		✓
6.	✓	

∩ D Do you hear e?
Class CD 1, Track 5

Audio Script

1.	tea	/tiᵏ/
2.	ten	/tɛn/
3.	toe	/toʷ/
4.	cheese	/tʃiᵏz/
5.	two	/tuʷ/
6.	please	/pliᵏz/

Answer Key

	Yes	No
1.	✓	
2.		✓
3.		✓
4.	✓	
5.		✓
6.	✓	

∩ E Do you hear *i*?

Audio Script

1.	ice	/aʸs/
2.	tie	/taʸ/
3.	say	/seʸ/
4.	hi	/haʸ/
5.	fries	/fraʸz/
6.	cheese	/tʃiʸz/

Answer Key

	Yes	No
1.	✓	
2.	✓	
3.		✓
4.	✓	
5.	✓	
6.		✓

∩ F Do you hear *o*?
Class CD 1, Track 7

Audio Script

1.	cone	/koʷn/
2.	so	/soʷ/
3.	go	/goʷ/
4.	cake	/keʸk/
5.	boat	/boʷt/
6.	fries	/fraʸz/

Answer Key

	Yes	No
1.	✓	
2.	✓	
3.	✓	
4.		✓
5.	✓	
6.		✓

∩ G Do you hear *u*?
Class CD 1, Track 8

Audio Script

1.	cube	/kyuʷb/
2.	me	/miʸ/
3.	cute	/kyuʷt/
4.	use	/yuʷz/
5.	cone	/koʷn/
6.	juice	/dʒuʷs/

Answer Key

	Yes	No
1.	✓	
2.		✓
3.	✓	
4.	✓	
5.		✓
6.	✓	

∩ H Which word is different?
Class CD 1, Track 9

To introduce students to this type of exercise, practice it on the board. Write the letters "X," "Y," and "Z," with two rows of answer blanks underneath them. Say a set of three words (e.g., "cake," "cake," "tea"), and point to the blanks under the "X," "Y," and "Z" as you say them. Have a student put a check mark under the correct letter for the word that was different (in this case, under "Z" for the word "tea"). Give another example, such as "hi," "he," "hi." Then proceed with the task.

Audio Script

1. see, see, say
   /siʸ/, /siʸ/, /seʸ/
2. tea, tea, tie
   /tiʸ/, /tiʸ/, /taʸ/
3. me, my, me
   /miʸ/, /maʸ/, /miʸ/
4. way, we, way
   /weʸ/, /wiʸ/, /weʸ/
5. plays, please, plays
   /pleʸz/, /pliʸz/, /pleʸz/
6. so, so, say
   /soʷ/, /soʷ/, /seʸ/
7. two, toe, two
   /tuʷ/, /toʷ/, /tuʷ/
8. why, we, why
   /waʸ/, /wiʸ/, /waʸ/

Answer Key

	X	Y	Z
1.			✓
2.			✓
3.		✓	
4.		✓	
5.		✓	
6.			✓
7.		✓	
8.		✓	

🎧 I Saying the alphabet vowel sounds
Class CD 1, Track 10

In this task, students will hear the alphabet vowel sounds and encounter their symbols for the first time. These sounds are exactly the same as the names of most of the letters. The only slightly different one is the sound for the vowel *u*, as the name of the letter includes an on-glide /ʸ/ sound before the /uʷ/ sound. Students will see a note about this in Unit 2, Task C, on page 8 of the Student's Book, so only explain this difference at this point if students ask about it and you think they should not wait until Unit 2.

The shape (rounding or spreading) of the lips and the timing of this movement are crucial to pronouncing these vowels clearly. If you look at a Spanish-speaker's mouth just about to say "si" (/siʸ/), the lips will be spread before the sound /s/ is begun. A native English speaker's mouth, just about to say "see" (/siʸ/), will not spread the lips until the end of the /iʸ/ vowel, or the part of the vowel known as the "/ʸ/ *off-glide*." Tell students to smile when they say vowels that end in a /ʸ/ off-glide. Many other languages do not have /ʸ/ or /ʷ/ off-glide endings for vowels, so it is a foreign concept to many students.

🎧 J Key words for the alphabet vowel sounds
Class CD 1, Track 11

Key words help students remember the sound quality of these vowel sounds, so these same key words will be repeated frequently throughout the early units. Food words are used as a main topic in the early units of this book because food is a popular subject and many students will already know some of this vocabulary.

> **Teaching tip** To help reinforce the vowel sounds in the key words, make a chart of the vowels and key words and display it in the classroom. Students might like to make their own personal charts. As students progress through the course, they can add other words that have similar sounds.

Answer Key

Letter	Key word
a	cake
e	tea
i	ice
o	cone
u	cube

🎧 K Food
Class CD 1, Track 12

Before listening, point to the pictures and say the words for your students, e.g., "cheeseburger," "French fries," "ice cream cones," etc.

🎧 L Music of English
Class CD 1, Track 13

Throughout the book, Music of English tasks teach students the **rhythm** and **intonation of English** (the music of the language). Students need to hear these sentences several times to get an accurate acoustic imprint in their minds before they are asked to speak. Either play the audio or model the sentences yourself. If you model, be sure to lengthen the vowel sounds in "cake" and "tea" to introduce students to this aspect of English rhythm: The **stressed syllable** in the **most important word** in a sentence has a lengthened vowel. Then ask the class to say the words with you as you speak. If they "mirror" in this way (speaking in unison with the model), they will be absorbing the music of the language accurately.

> **Teaching tip** Here is an interesting "saturation" method used by a teacher of Swedish pronunciation, Olle Kjellin, M.D., to help his students learn the rhythm of their new language. Ask your students to listen without saying anything as you repeat a sample sentence out loud 10 to 15 times. As you repeat, gradually exaggerate your body movements more each time to accompany and reinforce the rhythm and stress. Finally, ask the whole class to say the sentence in chorus with you, mirroring your speech, and repeating many times. You can vary the repetitions by asking only half the class, or a small group, to repeat, then returning to the whole class. Each "quality repetition" reinforces the strength of the long-term memory, giving students a template of spoken English that can be referred to later as you teach the various elements of the template.

Unit 1 Quiz is available on page 72.

2 The Two Vowel Rule

How do you spell "time"?

Unit overview

In this unit, students practice saying the alphabet sounds they listened to in Unit 1. Then they learn the Two Vowel Rule, which will help them guess how to pronounce words with two vowel letters.

A Saying the letters of the alphabet
Class CD 1, Track 14

In this task, learners repeat the letters of the alphabet. Most language courses begin with a brief presentation of the alphabet, and then move on quickly to other topics. However, learning to understand and saying the names of the letters are important skills that merit plenty of attention. This is because spelling out loud is such a useful tool for correcting misunderstandings. Even advanced students may be uncertain about the names of certain letters. Here are some that are confusing:

Letter	Name
a	/e^y/
e	/i^y/
i	/ɑ^y/
g	/dʒi^y/
j	/dʒe^y/

Sometimes students simply avoid saying difficult letters such as **-w-** (/'dʌb•əl•yu^w/ or /'dʌb•ə•yu^w/), **-x-** (/ɛks/), and **-y-** (/wɑ^y/).

> **Teaching tip** For additional work with alphabet letters, students can copy the alphabet onto separate pieces of paper and give them to another student to arrange in order.
>
> Sequencing the letters is a difficult task, even for students whose first language uses a Roman alphabet. Even though the letters may look familiar, they may be in a different order or have a different sound in a student's first language. These kinds of differences can make the use of a dictionary frustrating for learners, so it is important for students to learn the names and order of the English alphabet letters early on.

B The Two Vowel Rule
Class CD 1, Track 15

This task introduces a simple decoding rule that will help students figure out how a particular spelling might be pronounced. The first crucial concept is to understand the difference between *letter* and *sound*. In some languages, they are the same, but in English the letters, especially vowel letters, can have very different sounds. This rule gives a simple way to guess if the vowel letter will be pronounced the same as the name of the letter of the alphabet. According to the Two Vowel Rule, when there are two vowel letters in a word, the first vowel letter says its alphabet name, and the second letter is silent. The rule is given for short, one-syllable words in this unit. But the rule is expanded to multi-syllabic words when students learn about *syllables* in Unit 3 and *stress* (*strong syllables*) in Unit 5.

There are exceptions to this rule, but it is true often enough to help students overcome the feeling that English spelling, especially vowels, is an insurmountable obstacle.

A chart of the percent of time these rules work is given in Appendix C on page 132 of the Student's Book. These percentages can encourage students to believe the rules are worth learning.

For reference, here are some of the exceptions:

1. Sometimes the letters **-y-** and **-w-** act like vowels. When these letters immediately follow another vowel within a syllable, they activate the Two Vowel Rule:
   /e^y/ pay, say, play, stay
   /o^w/ show, slow, grow, bowl
2. The letter **-y-** sometimes sounds like /ɑ^y/: "shy," "why," "try," "my," "apply," "type." The letter **-y-** can also sound like /i^y/: "city," "pretty," "soapy," "sunny," "company."
3. The Two Vowel Rule does not work for the vowel combinations **-au-**, **-ou-**, or **-oi-**, as in "auto," "out," and "oil."

After students have listened to the words in step 1, write "make" on the board. Read the direction line in step 2, and model "underlining" the first vowel. Then have students complete the task.

For step 3, read the rule out loud to the students. Then have them identify the first and second vowels in each of the key words in the box and practice saying the key words with you.

Answer Key

1. m<u>a</u>ke
2. r<u>i</u>ce
3. t<u>ea</u>
4. p<u>ie</u>
5. h<u>o</u>me
6. c<u>u</u>be
7. s<u>oa</u>p
8. <u>u</u>se

C Words that end in the vowel letter -e-
Class CD 1, Track 16

Tasks C and D demonstrate two different applications of the Two Vowel Rule. In this task, students see how the rule applies when the second vowel is a final **-e-**. In the words in Task D, the two vowel letters are next to each other, and the second vowel letters vary.

D Words with two vowel letters together
Class CD 1, Track 17

This task helps solidify students' understanding of the term "vowel letter." As they listen, they should focus their attention on the first vowel letter, the one that most often determines the pronunciation of the word.

E Which vowel letter says its name?

To warm up, write several of the words on the board. Have students come up and underline the first vowel letter and pronounce the word. Then have students do the task individually.

Answer Key

1. m<u>a</u>de	p<u>ai</u>d	n<u>a</u>me	ch<u>a</u>nge	c<u>a</u>ke	J<u>a</u>ne	J<u>a</u>ke
2. cr<u>ea</u>m	pl<u>ea</u>se	s<u>ee</u>	ch<u>ee</u>se	thr<u>ee</u>	P<u>e</u>te	m<u>ee</u>t
3. t<u>i</u>me	s<u>i</u>ze	r<u>i</u>ce	l<u>i</u>ke	wr<u>i</u>te	b<u>i</u>ke	M<u>i</u>ke
4. s<u>oa</u>k	c<u>o</u>ne	b<u>oa</u>t	sm<u>o</u>ke	J<u>oe</u>	b<u>o</u>ne	h<u>o</u>me
5. c<u>u</u>te	c<u>u</u>be	tr<u>ue</u>	fr<u>ui</u>t	S<u>ue</u>	d<u>ue</u>	m<u>u</u>le

F Which vowel sound is it?
Class CD 1, Track 18

Here students practice discriminating between the five *alphabet vowel sounds*. If students need help getting started on step 2, copy the chart and vowel letters onto the board. Do some of the words as a class before students work individually.

Answer Key

/e^{y}/ cake	/i^{y}/ tea	/ɑ^{y}/ ice	/o^{w}/ cone	/u^{w}/ cube
came	meat	like	soap	tune
made	meal	mile	close	cue
rain	cheese			

G Music of English
Class CD 1, Track 19

This Music of English box prepares students for Task H.

If you model these sentences for your students, be sure to lengthen the vowel in "time" in the question and when you say the letter **-e-** in the answer. This will make a good model of the rhythm, as well as the melody. Do not slow down, because that will tend to alter the musical signals that are crucial to the sentence.

Note: After students listen to the audio and repeat the sentences, have them repeat the exchange as a whole piece, to show how the meanings of the sentences are linked.

H Pair work: Asking how to spell words
Class CD 1, Track 20

Spelling out loud is an important skill for students who have trouble being understood. That is why practicing these questions and answers is so important. They will be used in exercises throughout the Student's Book.

When spelling out loud, each letter is like a separate syllable, and the final syllable of a series generally has a rise / fall intonation, to signify "end of list." To model this, write several words on the board. Spell each word with a rise / fall intonation on the last letter, and then have the students repeat it with you.

I Pair work: How do you spell "cheese"?

Pair work practice keeps everybody in the class working, either concentrating on saying the sentence correctly or hearing it accurately. This sort of practice also lets the students focus on each other, instead of the teacher, which lowers the tension involved in speaking. Circulate around the room to check on students' work.

After reading the directions, model the task. Take the part of Student A and choose someone in the class to take the part of Student B. Act out choosing a word from the box (without Student B seeing you point) and asking the question. Have Student B answer your question, and then ask you a question.

When doing the task, both students should look at the list of words. Try to have them concentrate on accurate pronunciation, rather than spelling from memory. Make sure the students choose words at random, rather than going down the columns in order. A random approach keeps the listening partner alert. Students may benefit by trying the exercise with more than one partner.

J Spelling game

If possible, put the grid on the board – as a poster or projected from a computer – so that students focus on the spelling and look up while they are speaking. The grid should have letters down one side and numbers across the top.

Students take turns challenging the other team by saying a letter and number combination, such as "E-4." A student from the other team must spell the word in that cell of the grid and then pronounce it. One point can be given for every correct answer, or one point each can be awarded for correct spelling and correct pronunciation.

Unit 2 Quiz is available on page 73.

3 | Syllables

How many syllables are in "city"?

Unit overview

Unit 3 focuses students' attention on *syllables*. Students learn to listen to syllables, to tap them out and finally to count them. This lays the foundation for later units in which students will learn to identify the *strong* and *weak syllables* in words and phrases (Units 5 and 6, respectively).

Syllable number is an important topic because English learners often add or drop syllables according to the rules of their first language. This can cause serious intelligibility problems when, for example, "school" becomes "eschool" or "sekolah," "government" becomes "gahment," or "Yesterday I rented an apartment" becomes "Yest'day I rent' 'partment."

🎧 A Syllables
Class CD 1, Track 21

Before starting, point to the pictures and say the words "cheeseburger," "milkshake," and "banana." Then clap or tap out the syllables as you say them again.

If students want a definition of syllable, you can say that each syllable has a *vowel sound*. However, this is a complicated abstraction, so it is better to teach syllable kinesthetically as a physical sensation, like a beat or tap.

🎧 B Tapping the syllables
Class CD 1, Track 22

After students listen to each word, have them tap out the syllables they heard. By tapping out the syllables, students feel the physical sensation of the rhythm and succession of syllables. If they are reluctant to tap with their fingers while counting syllables, they can be encouraged to count by tapping a foot or simply by touching thumb to fingers.

Note: Some speakers pronounce "chocolate" as /'tʃak•lɛt/ (or /'tʃɔk•lət/), or with three syllables as /'tʃak•ə•lət/, but the most common pronunciation in American English is with two syllables. Many other languages use four syllables for this word.

🎧 C Counting syllables
Class CD 1, Track 23

Because the rhythm of our speech is deeply connected to our sense of who we are and what group we belong

to, students are sometimes uneasy about working on rhythm. A relaxed class atmosphere can help reduce this uneasiness. In some classes, students enjoy "dancing" exercises, where they can stand up and move various parts of the body (hand, head, foot, elbow, knee, etc.) to help count syllables.

Audio Script

1.	cola	/'koʷ•lə/
2.	city	/'sɪt•iʸ/
3.	cream	/kriʸm/
4.	creamy	/'kriʸ•miʸ/
5.	ice cream	/'aʸs kriʸm/
6.	salad	/'sæl•əd/
7.	cheese	/tʃiʸz/
8.	cheeses	/tʃiʸ•zəz/
9.	six	/sɪks/
10.	sixty	/'sɪks•tiʸ/

Answer Key

1.	2	(cola)
2.	2	(city)
3.	1	(cream)
4.	2	(creamy)
5.	2	(ice cream)
6.	2	(salad)
7.	1	(cheese)
8.	2	(cheeses)
9.	1	(six)
10.	2	(sixty)

🎧 D Which word is different?
Class CD 1, Track 24

Here students listen for syllable number to determine which word is different. Students were introduced to this format in Unit 1, Task H, but it may be helpful to review how it is done. Read the direction line and the three words shown next to item 1, the example. Draw attention to the checkmark in column Z. Then play the audio or read the script to the students.

1. sit, sit, city
   /sɪt/, /sɪt/, /ˈsɪt•iʸ/

2. pen, penny, pen
   /pɛn/, /ˈpɛn•iʸ/, /pɛn/

3. icy, icy, ice
   /ˈaʸ•siʸ/, /ˈaʸ•siʸ/, /aʸs/

4. cream, cream, creamy
   /kriʸm/, /kriʸm/, /ˈkriʸ•miʸ/

5. cola, coal, cola
   /ˈkoʷ•lə/, /koʷl/, /ˈkoʷ•lə/

6. shake, shake, shaker
   /ʃeʸk/, /ʃeʸk/, /ˈʃeʸ•kər/

7. soap, soap, soapy
   /soʷp/, /soʷp/, /ˈsoʷ•piʸ/

8. lemon, lemonade, lemon
   /ˈlɛm•ən/, /lɛm•əˈneʸd/, /ˈlɛm•ən/

9. cues, cues, excuse
   /kyuʷz/, /kyuʷz/, /ɛkˈskyuʷz/

10. six, sixty, six
    /sɪks/, /ˈsɪks•tiʸ/, /sɪks/

Answer Key

	X	Y	Z
1.			✓
2.		✓	
3.			✓
4.			✓
5.		✓	
6.			✓
7.			✓
8.		✓	
9.			✓
10.		✓	

E Pair work: One or two syllables?

It is important to prepare students for pair work by going over the instructions and doing the examples with them. As students work in pairs, move around the class and help as needed. After students have finished, call out words from the task, and have students hold up their fingers for the number of syllables.

Syllable counting is important not only for saying words clearly, but also for grammatical accuracy. The short *structure words* or affixes that students tend to leave out of their speech and writing are often grammatical markers ("-ing," "-ed," "is," "to," "the," etc.). These small but important elements are hard to hear in spoken English because they are systematically said less clearly in natural speech. Increased awareness of syllable count can serve as a reminder to include these small words and word endings.

> **Teaching tip** Dictation is an excellent technique for checking your students' accuracy in listening. Ask them to close their books, and then dictate a series of words from the list in this task, scrambling the order given in the Student's Book. Then check their writing, or have them check each other's accuracy. This will verify that they are actually paying attention to the number of syllables. After some continued work with syllable number, use dictation to check again (perhaps at the end of this unit).

F Tapping syllables in words
Class CD 1, Track 25

Here students listen to a list of words two times. The second time they listen, they should cover the list of words and tap out the syllables of each word after they hear it. Then have them write the number of syllables.

To check their work at the end, have students give the answer and then tap out the syllables as they say the word.

> **Teaching tip** Ask students how many syllables are in a word each time you introduce a new vocabulary item. This seems to help with both spelling and memory of pronunciation.

Answer Key

1. banana	1. 3
2. sandwich	2. 2
3. milkshake	3. 2
4. painted	4. 2
5. rented	5. 2
6. closed	6. 1
7. opened	7. 2
8. cleaned	8. 1

G Tapping syllables in groups of words
Class CD 1, Track 26

In this task, students progress to listening to and tapping out syllables in phrases.

After they hear each phrase on the audio, they should repeat it while tapping out the syllables.

🎧 H Music of English
Class CD 1, Track 27

"How many syllables are in 'city'?" is a very long sentence for beginners, containing ten syllables and including the difficult word "syllables." If students try to recite this whole sentence, they are apt to become more and more uncertain as they move forward. You can help them master this sentence by using the technique of "backward buildup." Have students work on "in 'city'?" first, concentrating on correct rhythm and melody in this phrase alone. Then work on "are in 'city'?" When they can say this with confidence, lengthen it to "syllables are in 'city'?" When these seven syllables are said easily and correctly, lengthen it to "How many syllables are in 'city'?" At each step, the students are reciting in the direction of greater confidence.

Teaching tip   To vary the task, students can practice this musical exercise individually, in groups, or as a class. It is also helpful for students to follow the pitch line, either by tracing the line in the book with their finger or by drawing the pitch line in the air as they speak.

I Pair work: How many syllables are in "forty"?

Warm up for the task by doing the examples with the class. After pair work, have individual students ask and answer questions for the class.

Answer Key

cit•y	sal•ad	bur•ger	class	va•nill•a
for•ty	com•pu•ter	co•ffee	milk•shake	cu•cum•ber

🎧 J The Two Vowel Rule for syllables
Class CD 1, Track 28

The Two Vowel Rule is repeated here, but "short word" has been changed to "syllable." This is to help students realize that the rule works for words with more than one syllable. Again, there are many exceptions, but the rule works well enough to serve as a useful guide for beginners, giving them more confidence in decoding English pronunciation.

Teaching tip   Here are some more challenging words for additional practice. Write the words in columns on the board, and have students repeat them after you. Have students come to the board and underline the syllable with two vowels, and then circle the first vowel.

/e^y/

waitress	/'we^y•trɛs/
arrangement	/ə're^{y}ndʒ•mənt/

/i^y/

teacher	/'ti^y•tʃər/
easy	/'i^y•zi^y/

/ɑ^y/

alive	/ə'lɑ^{y}v/
decide	/də'sɑ^{y}d/
advice	/əd'vɑ^{y}s/

/o^w/

telephone	/'tɛl•ə•fo^{w}n/
oatmeal	/'o^{w}t•mi^{y}l/

/u^w/

avenue	/'æv•ə•nu^w/
continue	/kən•'tɪn•yu^w/
Tuesday	/'tu^{w}z•di^y/ or /'tu^{w}z•de^y/

🎧 K Music of English
Class CD 1, Track 29

This exchange prepares students for pair work in Task L.

L Pair work: How do you spell "city"?

This type of task provides lots of practice with the names of the letters and the useful skill of spelling out loud. Make sure students are not just asking questions **a** and **b** in sequence, as this provides little challenge for their partners.

If students are relatively advanced, have the answering students listen with the words covered up. Lower-level students may need to read both sentences to themselves first, so that they can understand the meaning of the alternate choices. Use the illustrations provided to help them understand the vocabulary.

The main purpose of this task is to help students notice the difference between similar and confusing words by noticing the number of syllables in the words. The concept of "syllable" may not fit their first languages, so this work is helpful. The task should be as challenging as possible, within the ability of the students to succeed. This makes it like a game.

M Food game

If the teams have difficulty getting started, help them think of some food words as a class. Write them on the board, and count the syllables.

For more practice after the game, here are some additional words to give students. Students can write the words in the correct columns on the board. To check spelling, have them ask you, "How do you spell…?"

salad	/'sæl•əd/
potato	/pə'te^y•to^w/
asparagus	/ə'spær•ə•gəs/
peas	/pi^{y}z/
butter	/'bʌt•ər/
tomato	/tə'me^y•to^w/
avocado	/ɑ•və'kɑ•do^w/
corn	/kɔrn/
spaghetti	/spə'gɛt•i^y/
grapes	/gre^{y}ps/
carrots	/'kɛr•əts/
cucumber	/'kyu^w•kʌm•bər/

eggs	/ɛgz/
raisins	/'re^y•zənz/
toast	/to^{w}st/
chicken	/'tʃɪk•ən/
cheeseburger	/'tʃi^{y}z•bər•gər/
beef	/bi^{y}f/
tuna	/'tu^w•nə/
fish	/fɪʃ/
muffin	/'mʌf•ən/
celery	/'sɛl•ə•ri^y/
beans	/bi^{y}nz/
melons	/'mɛl•ənz/

N Review: The Two Vowel Rule

This is the first time students are asked to notice that the vowel sound is the peak of the key word – or the "peak of the pronunciation pyramid." Because this vowel must be said clearly and because the same vowel letter can have a different sound, it is helpful for students to begin to recognize the special symbol for that sound.

In future pyramid review tasks, students will be asked to complete the other levels of the pyramid, gradually focusing on the other key elements of pronunciation as they are presented and practiced in the units. In this introductory task, the students are only being asked to notice the relationship of the symbol to the word.

Unit 3 Quiz is available on page 74.

4 The One Vowel Rule
Linking with /n/

What does "less" mean?
How do you say S - H - A - K - E?

Unit overview

In Unit 4, students contrast the Two Vowel Rule they learned in Unit 2 with the One Vowel Rule. This is basically a contrast between the classic minimal pair vowels (e.g., "ship" / "sheep"), but in a new perspective.

Clear Speech From the Start differs from the traditional approach to teaching **vowel sounds**, which are often referred to as "long" and "short." It is true that an **alphabet vowel** said by itself (out of context) sounds longer than a **relative** (short) **vowel** simply because the alphabet vowels have a /ʸ/ or /ʷ/ **off-glide** that takes time to say. (Relative vowels do not have off-glides.) But vowels are not said by themselves, and in the actual context of a word, short vowels can take longer to say than the long ones.

Also, from a teaching standpoint, if the terms "long" and "short" are used to mean vowel quality (e.g., "made" /meʸd/ and "mad" /mæd/), it will be confusing for the student if these same terms are used later when discussing the length of the vowel in a **stressed syllable** (e.g., "banana") in Unit 5.

This book saves the terms "long" and "short" to refer only to real timing length when the vowels are said in actual running speech. This distinction is presented in Units 5 and 6.

Note: The alphabet letter **-a-** has another relative sound, /ɔ/ (e.g., "call," "ball," "mall," "fall"), but it is less common.

Task A introduces the vocabulary term "relative." Task B practices using the Two Vowel Rule with the Green family. Task C then introduces the concept of relative vowel sounds with the Red Family.

Unit 4 also introduces the concept of linking, which is developed throughout the book. Linking, which refers to the way the final sound of a word connects to the initial sound of the word that follows it, is a key characteristic of spoken English. In this unit, learners listen to and practice words linked with /**n**/, anticipating linking with /**m**/ in Unit 5.

🎧 A The Green family and the Two Vowel Rule
Class CD 1, Track 30

1. The purpose of this family tree is to practice the Two Vowel Rule and prepare students for the idea of relatives, which will be useful when they learn the One Vowel Rule and the concept of a relative vowel sound in Task C.

   Students will hear sentences describing the relationships of people in the Green family. Students can point to the names as they hear them.

> *Audio Script*
>
> Grandfather Green and Grandmother Green
> Their children are Mike and Eve.
> Jean and Mike are married.
> Their children are Joe and Pete.
> Joe and Joan are married.
> Their children are Kate, May, and June.
> Eve and Dave are married.
> Their children are Sue and Jane.

2. Read the information in the box to remind students about the Two Vowel Rule. It is essential that they have firm acoustic images in mind for the alphabet vowel sounds before presenting the contrasting relative vowel sounds.

> **Teaching tip**   The family trees in Tasks A and C could be put on the board or on a screen and used for practice with relationship terms ("sister," "grandparents," "children," etc.).
>
> As a good reminder of the One and Two Vowel Rules, you could put the family trees on a poster and display them in the classroom for the remainder of the course.

B Pair work: Questions about the Green family

Make sure students know the gender of the names in the Green family so that they will know which people are sons, sisters, brothers, etc. "Mike," "Joe," "Pete," and "Dave" are the male names, and the others are the female names.

Answer Key

1. Pete
2. Sue
3. Grandmother Green
4. Joe
5. Mike
6. May and June
7. Eve
8. Joe and Pete

C The Red family and the One Vowel Rule
Class CD 1, Track 31

Now, with the word "relative" clear, and having reviewed the alphabet vowel sounds, it is time to introduce the relative vowel sounds.

1. As students listen to the audio for this exercise, they will focus on relative vowel sounds. After students have done the task, explain that relative vowel sound means that this sound is a "relative" of the alphabet vowel sound. The alphabet vowel sound and the relative vowel sound are related because they are alternative pronunciations of the same vowel letter. The actual quality of a relative vowel sound must be learned by hearing it many times. Describing the position of the tongue is not as helpful as giving students opportunities to listen and to develop an acoustic imprint in their minds.

The relative vowels are more common in spoken English than the alphabet vowels, but they are more difficult for students to learn. That is why the Two Vowel Rule was presented first. Both of these rules have many exceptions, but they work well enough to help students decide how a printed word is likely to be pronounced.

The usefulness of this vowel rule is shown in Appendix C, in the chart of percentages on page 133 of the Student's Book.

Audio Script

Grandfather Red and Grandmother Red
Sam and Jim are their children.
Jenny and Sam are married.
Ann, Pat, and Ben are their children.
Ted and Ann are married.
Russ, Bill, and Tom are their children.
Jim and Jan are married.
Zack and Mack are their children.
Mack and Kitty are married.
Jeff, Gus, and John are their children.

2. Go over the One Vowel Rule with students. It can be helpful to tell them that very short words that end in a vowel do not always follow this rule (e.g., "hi," "me," "she," "go").

Students may want to know the gender of the names. "Pat" could be either a male or female name. "Jenny," "Ann," "Jan," and "Kitty" are female names, and the other names are male.

D Words with relative vowel sounds
Class CD 1, Track 32

In this exercise, students will hear relative vowel sounds. Don't ask them to repeat the words. They should just listen at this point.

E Key words for the relative vowel sounds
Class CD 1, Track 33

As for the key words presented for the alphabet vowel sounds, these key words should help students remember the quality of the relative vowel sounds.

Answer Key

Vowel letter	Relative sound key word
a	man
e	men
i	pill
o	pot
u	sun

F The difference between alphabet vowel sounds and relative vowel sounds
Class CD 1, Track 34

Before students listen to the audio, remind them to pay attention to the differences between the alphabet vowels and relative vowels they will hear.

🎧 G Do you hear /æ/?
Class CD 1, Track 35

Audio Script

1.	man	/mæn/
2.	main	/me^{y}n/
3.	Sam	/sæm/
4.	same	/se^{y}m/
5.	can	/kæn/
6.	mad	/mæd/

Answer Key

	Yes	No
1.	✓	
2.		✓
3.	✓	
4.		✓
5.	✓	
6.	✓	

🎧 H Do you hear /ɛ/?
Class CD 1, Track 36

Audio Script

1.	men	/mɛn/
2.	mean	/mi^{y}n/
3.	chess	/tʃɛs/
4.	lease	/li^{y}s/
5.	cheese	/tʃi^{y}z/
6.	ten	/tɛn/

Answer Key

	Yes	No
1.	✓	
2.		✓
3.	✓	
4.		✓
5.		✓
6.	✓	

🎧 I Do you hear /ɪ/?
Class CD 1, Track 37

Audio Script

1.	pill	/pɪl/
2.	file	/fɑ^{y}l/
3.	skin	/skɪn/
4.	pine	/pɑ^{y}n/
5.	wish	/wɪʃ/
6.	wise	/wɑ^{y}z/

Answer Key

	Yes	No
1.	✓	
2.		✓
3.	✓	
4.		✓
5.	✓	
6.		✓

🎧 J Do you hear /ɑ/?
Class CD 1, Track 38

Audio Script

1.	pot	/pɑt/
2.	Joan	/dʒo^{w}n/
3.	rod	/rɑd/
4.	rope	/ro^{w}p/
5.	hot	/hɑt/
6.	John	/dʒɑn/

Answer Key

	Yes	No
1.	✓	
2.		✓
3.	✓	
4.		✓
5.	✓	
6.	✓	

∩ K Do you hear /ʌ/?
Class CD 1, Track 39

Audio Script

1. sun	/sʌn/
2. tube	/tuʷb/
3. club	/klʌb/
4. cub	/kʌb/
5. blue	/bluʷ/
6. tub	/tʌb/

Answer Key

	Yes	No
1.	✓	
2.		✓
3.	✓	
4.	✓	
5.		✓
6.	✓	

∩ L Which word is different?
Class CD 1, Track 40

Here students listen for vowel sounds to determine which word is different. Read the direction line and the three words shown next to item 1. Draw attention to the check mark in column Y. Then play the audio or read the script.

Audio Script

1. mate, mat, mate
   /meʸt/, /mæt/, /meʸt/
2. pine, pin, pine
   /paʸn/, /pɪn/, /paʸn/
3. mean, men, men
   /miʸn/, /mɛn/, /mɛn/
4. hop, hope, hop
   /hɑp/, /hoʷp/, /hɑp/
5. at, ate, ate
   /æt/, /eʸt/, /eʸt/
6. ice, ice, is
   /aʸs/, /aʸs/, /ɪz/
7. cute, cut, cute
   /kyuʷt/, /kʌt/, /kyuʷt/

Answer Key

	X	Y	Z
1.		✓	
2.		✓	
3.	✓		
4.		✓	
5.	✓		
6.			✓
7.		✓	

∩ M Listening to vowel sounds
Class CD 1, Track 41

Students often worry when they do not know the meaning of all the words they see, but try to get students to pay attention to the spelling, not the meaning, in this task. The purpose of this task is to help students learn to guess the vowel sounds by listening and looking at the spelling. Discussing vocabulary takes away time that would be better spent mastering the connection between sound and spelling.

∩ N Which vowel sound do you hear?
Class CD 1, Track 42

1. As students listen to the audio, they can put a check mark next to the words they think have alphabet vowel sounds. This will help them when they do step 2.
2. Have students write the words in the correct boxes. They can do this in pairs or groups. Write the chart on the board, and check answers as a class by asking, "What words go in this box?"

Answer Key

/eʸ/	/iʸ/	/aʸ/	/oʷ/	/uʷ/
made	cheese	ride	road	cute
shake	teen	pine	hope	rule
main	lease	ice	coast	cube

/æ/	/ɛ/	/ɪ/	/ɑ/	/ʌ/
mad	less	rid	hop	fun
shack	chess	is	hot	cut
man	ten	pin	rod	cub

⌒ O Music of English
Class CD 1, Track 43

"What does 'less' mean?" is another useful "song" for beginners. "How do you say 'S-H-A-K-E'?" helps students gradually develop the skill of spelling out loud.

The letters in a spelled word are said like a series of any kind, and the signal for "last one" is a rise and then a fall. This is also true for acronyms (e.g., CNN, BBC, VIP, etc.) and lists of any kind.

If you are modeling these sentences, lengthen the vowel sound in "less" and "lease," and the final letter -e- in "S-H-A-K-E." "Less," "lease," and the final letter in a spelled word are the most important parts of these sentences, and as such they have longer vowels. Unit 5 will explain this for the students, but in the meantime they need to hear you say the sentences spoken with accurate English rhythm.

> **Teaching tip** Since many repetitions helps increase exact rhythmic control, vary the repetition drill by asking students to do it with *whispering* instead of speaking. Whispering concentrates the mind because it is such a change, and rhythm can be heard quite well without the voice.
>
> "Walkabout" is another useful technique: Have students circle the room, walking to the rhythm as they say the sentences many times. You can step out of the circle and listen to the students as they go around. When students say the words "less" or "lease," they should take an extra long step. Then have students take a separate step for each letter of the word "S-H-A-K-E," with an extra long step for the final -e-. For full effect, the walking / talking needs a lot of repetition.

P Pair work: How do you say S-H-A-K-E?

After reading the directions, ask students to read the examples. Then model the task by taking the part of Student A and choosing someone in the class to take the part of Student B. Act out choosing a question to ask, then have Student B answer your question. Confirm or correct the answer, then have Student B ask you a question. Finally, put students into pairs, and have them take turns asking and answering the questions. Make sure students choose questions at random to keep the task interesting.

Short-form answers are given here, rather than full sentences, because that is how people usually talk. Also, short, easy-to-say responses are easier to produce and will help this sort of pair work go smoothly.

⌒ Q Linking with /n/
Class CD 1, Track 44

This exercise introduces students to the concept of linking. Many languages have a brief silence between all words and, in written English, words are separated with a white space. However, in spoken English, the final sound of a word often links to the initial sound of the next.

It is important to practice linking for two main reasons. First, listening comprehension is improved when students practice hearing words run together. Second, linking is an aid to fluency; when students link words in their own speech, they sound more natural and can begin to express themselves in word groups, rather than in unnaturally separated words.

There are other good reasons for students to practice linking. Many languages do not allow final consonants, and students need practice concentrating on consonant endings.

Linking is also a good way to help students learn to pronounce difficult sounds, because it effectively moves word-final sounds into word-initial position. Often, students will have less trouble hearing and pronouncing a difficult sound at the beginning of a word than at the end. In the first part of the task, the final /n/ at the end of the first word is linked to a word that starts with a vowel sound because it is easier to hear the linking when it involves a following vowel sound. In the second part of the task, the final /n/ of the first word is linked to the initial /n/ of the second word.

1. When you model the linked words in this task, draw out the linking sound in an exaggerated way, to focus attention on the link.
2. Point out to students that the letter -k- is silent in the word "know."

⌒ R More linking with /n/
Class CD 1, Track 45

This is the first task in which students actually have the opportunity to practice linking. A useful approach is to have students use their index fingers to draw a linking symbol (like the curved line that connects "Dan" and "is" in item 1) in the air as they say the linking /n/ sound in each sentence. Encourage students to exaggerate the linking sounds as they practice.

Another approach is to instruct students to bring their hands together just as they begin the linking sound. This physical effort requires close attention to the onset of linking, which increases focus on the linking use of the target sound.

S Game: What vowel sound does the letter have?

This task is meant to provide extra practice for some of the vowel sounds and, at the same time, to reinforce work done in Units 1 and 2 on pronouncing the names of the letters.

If you feel students need to listen to the alphabet again in order to do the task or to check their answers, you can read the letters out loud for them or play the audio for Unit 1 Task A.

Answer Key

/e^y/ cake	/i^y/ tea	/ɛ/ ten	/ɑ^y/ ice	/o^w/ cone	/u^w/ cube
a	b	f	i	o	q
h	c	l	y		u
j	d	m			w
k	e	n			
	g	s			
	p	x			
	t				
	v				
	z				

T Review: The One Vowel Rule

In this task, students are asked to recognize the vowel symbols at the peak of the pyramid and write the appropriate name underneath. This should help them associate the vowel sound to the spelling of the names.

Answer Key

1. Jan
2. Jen
3. Bill
4. Tom
5. Gus

Unit 4 Quiz is available on page 75.

5 Strong Syllables
Linking with /m/

What's that called?
What's it for?

Unit overview

In this unit, students learn the rules for *strong syllables*. The terms *strong* and *weak syllables* are used to introduce students to the concept of *stressed* and *unstressed* (or reduced) *syllables* because the terms "strong" and "weak" are less abstract.

Students need to practice lengthening some vowel sounds. This is in preparation for knowing which vowel to lengthen to make a syllable strong. This vowel is the peak of information in the *most important word,* introduced in Unit 7. Lengthening some vowels and not others is challenging for English learners because many other languages have relatively equal length for all syllables, and it is difficult for speakers of those languages to notice variable syllable length in English. Variable syllable length affects the rhythm of speech. Because rhythm of one's first language is the first thing a baby learns, and therefore has deep emotional meaning, it can be disturbing to students to alter their rhythm. This different rhythm may make them sound foreign to themselves, but being aware of syllable length is important for understanding word and sentence stress patterns, which are a central element of communication in spoken English.

After the work with syllable lengthening, this unit teaches *linking* with the consonant /**m**/, building on what students learned in Unit 4 about linking with /**n**/.

Finally, students learn to listen for the past tense ending of verbs spelled with -**ed** and then practice distinguishing whether or not there is actually an extra syllable.

A Strong syllables
Class CD 1, Track 46

1. Point out to students how the vowel letter at the center of the strong syllable is extra wide (stretched). This makes it easier for them to notice the extra length of the stressed syllable. Because a vowel is the center, or core, of a syllable, when the spoken vowel is lengthened, it makes the syllable longer and more prominent. This helps the listener notice the strong syllable. This system of variable lengthening is foreign to many learners, and therefore important to practice.

3. If you model the word "banana" for students, exaggerate the lengthened vowel so that students can hear it easily. Students can be helped to notice the stressed syllable by practicing saying the word, and moving their hands apart, or stretching a wide rubber band as they say the stressed syllable in a word like "banana." This can help them get a physical sense of this variable length. The rubber band just mimics the effort of concentration required. Using a rubber band also helps students get the idea of counting syllables, because they have to concentrate on when to stretch and when not to stretch.

Note: Use a wide rubber band. A thin rubber band does not convey the effort a student must make to adequately lengthen the vowel, and it is also apt to break.

B Listening for strong syllables
Class CD 1, Track 47

Students will listen for the strong (stressed) syllables in each word and underline the long vowel in that syllable. Some students may have difficulty noticing stress, especially if their first language has *fixed stress* that always falls on the same syllable, often the first, or the next to last. Unfortunately for learners, English stress does not have a fixed location, and there is no symbol in the written language that shows the stress, as there is in some other languages.

Since there are no simple, practical rules for placement of stress, the most useful approach is to teach students to listen for the extra length and *contrastive* clarity of the stressed vowels. The shortness and obscurity of vowels in weak syllables (taught in Unit 6) serve to contrastively highlight the length and clarity of stressed vowels in strong syllables. This is important because, if the word is chosen as the most important word in the sentence (taught in Unit 7), this lengthening of the vowel is the crucial signal that the listener must notice.

Students of English assume that the stress is unimportant, if they are even aware of the concept. They tend to ignore the little stress marks in their dictionaries. Far from unimportant, word-stress patterns are essential to clear communication in spoken English. A stress-pattern mistake can cause great confusion, especially if it is accompanied by any other kind of error, because it is hard for native English speakers to understand words that are stressed incorrectly.

Note: When you check the answers and come to the word "chocolate," remind students of the importance of the number of syllables. In some languages, this word is pronounced with four syllables.

C Saying strong syllables
Class CD 1, Track 48

Have students repeat the words they hear. They can use a rubber band to show syllable length, as they did in Task A.

Audio Script

1. sofa	/ˈsoʷ•fə/
2. blanket	/ˈblæŋ•kət/
3. carpet	/ˈkɑr•pət/
4. newspaper	/ˈnuʷs•peʸ•pər/
5. telephone	/ˈtɛl•ə•foʷn/
6. washing machine	/ˈwɑʃ•ɪŋ məˈʃiʸn/
7. refrigerator	/rɪˈfrɪdʒ•ə•reʸ•tər/
8. television	/ˈtɛl•ə•vɪʒ•ən/
9. freezer	/ˈfriʸ•zər/
10. alarm clock	/əˈlɑrm ˈklɑk/
11. can opener	/ˈkæn ˈoʷ•pə•nər/
12. vacuum cleaner	/ˈvæk•yuʷm ˈkliʸ•nər/
13. ceiling	/ˈsiʸ•lɪŋ/
14. bathtub	/ˈbæθ•tʌb/

D Strong syllables in sentences

This task presents the rules for strong syllables in a short sentence or word group – probably the most important feature of English pronunciation taught in this course. The key rule is introduced in step 2 on page 32 of the Student's Book: The vowel in the strong syllable of the most important word is extra long. When students learn to emphasize the most important word by lengthening the vowel in its strong syllable, they will have a major tool for improving the clarity of their English. This timing signal helps the listener notice where the pitch has changed and, therefore, understand which word is most important. This will be explained to students in Unit 7, but the Music of English boxes in Units 5 and 6 will give students practice using vowel length correctly.

Review the Strong Syllable Rule with students. This rule applies to words said in isolation, i.e., the word said alone is, by itself, a complete musical phrase. Then introduce Another Strong Syllable Rule, which is about words spoken together with other words in a word group.

Note: A *word group* is a short sentence, clause, or phrase. This is the same as the term *thought group*. *Word group* is used in *Clear Speech From the Start* because it is an easier concept and term for students at this level to grasp. *Thought group* is used in *Clear Speech*, the more advanced level book.

E Music of English
Class CD 1, Track 49

Before students listen to the audio, remind them that the stretched letters show which vowels they should lengthen.

The *contractions* "what's" and "it's" are the usual form in spoken English (but not in formal written English).

It is natural for students to lapse back into the rhythm of their first language when they have been focusing on other aspects of language or thinking about meaning. Be aware of this tendency, and, if it occurs, remind students about lengthening the vowel in the strong syllable of the most important word. It can be very helpful to occasionally refresh their awareness of rhythm by using choral repetition of the template, as a review. In choral recitation, students reinforce each other's sense of rhythm, as they tend to fall into rhythmic harmony with the group voice. This strengthens their sense of the variable length of syllables, which is so characteristic of English.

Note: After students have learned to say each sentence easily, have them practice the exchange as a whole piece again to show how the meanings and intonation patterns of the sentences are linked.

> **Teaching tip** One way to use English rhythm practice is with contractions. Students are often uneasy with saying contractions, but they need to learn to recognize them, and practice saying them helps listening comprehension.
>
> A good way to practice contractions is to write on the board the following (or other auxiliary contractions):
>
> | | |
> |---|---|
> | I am | I'm |
> | He is | He's |
> | They will | They'll |
>
> Lead half the class to say the first word ("I"), then lead the other half to say the second word ("am"), and then have the whole class say them both together ("I'm"). When done in a rhythmic chant, this is a powerful technique for practicing the difference in syllable number between the full, emphatic form and the more usual contracted form.

F Pair work: What's that called?

After reading the directions, model the task by taking the part of Student A and choosing someone in the class to take the part of Student B. It can be helpful to point to the pictures on page 33 of the Student's Book and have the class say the names of the objects in unison. Then put students into pairs, and have them take turns asking and answering the questions.

G Music of English
Class CD 1, Track 50

"What's it for?" is another useful fixed "song." The answer gives students good practice in noticing which word usually gets the emphasis.

H What's it for?
Class CD 1, Track 51

This practice will help prepare students for Task I.

I Pair work: What's it for?

After reading the instructions, model the examples in the box with a student. Then put students into pairs, and have them take turns asking and answering the question, "What's it for?" Remind students that all of the answers are in Task H.

For further practice, you can have students ask you about other items in the classroom. Write on the board "What's this / that called?" and "What's it for?" to help them. Then students can point to items and ask these questions.

J Review: Counting syllables

Have students write the number of syllables in the words. Then put the answers on the board so that they can check their work.

Answer Key	
1. Canada	3
2. sofa	2
3. blanket	2
4. telephone	3
5. paper towels	4 or 3
6. television	4
7. freezer	2
8. alarm clock	3
9. carpet	2
10. refrigerator	5

To extend the task, ask students to list some classroom items (or other common items) and count the syllables for those words. Here are some possible examples:

whiteboard	(2)
eraser	(3)
picture	(2)
map	(1)
backpack	(2)
women	(2)
men	(1)
window	(2)
dictionary	(4)
projector	(3)

K Past -ed ending
Class CD 1, Track 52

Tasks K, L, and M, which focus on the past tense ending -ed, should be useful for students who have begun to learn about this past tense form. However, the past tense ending may be too advanced for your students if they have not studied this tense yet. If this is the case, just ask them to count the syllables as they listen to Tasks K and L, without going on to explain the rules for pronouncing the -ed ending. Then skip Task M.

Make sure students tap two syllables for "rented" and "needed" and just one for "played" and "talked."

L Extra syllable or not?
Class CD 1, Track 53

2. The verbs "walked," "cleaned," and "closed" are the only ones that are one syllable.
3. The rules help students learn when the -ed ending adds an extra syllable.

Note: You might want to point out that "talk" /tɔk/ and "walk" /wɔk/ both have a silent letter -l-.

M Pair work: Yesterday or every day?

This task gives students practice listening for and pronouncing the past tense -ed ending in the context of whole sentences. It also reinforces students' understanding of how meaning is connected to form.

After reading the instructions, model the examples with a student. Then put students into pairs, and have them take turns saying either sentence **a** or **b** and responding with "every day" or "yesterday."

When they finish, you can consolidate by saying some additional sentences and having students respond as a whole class. For example:

We want a new car.
He used a backpack.
You washed the dishes.
We brush our teeth.

⌒ N Linking with /m/
Class CD 1, Track 54

Remind students that it is very important to practice linking because it will make their speech sound more natural and will improve their listening comprehension. Explain that, in normal English speech, words are run together rather than separated by silence.

Have students listen to the examples they hear in steps 1 and 2 and repeat the sentences they hear in step 3 at least two times. Encourage students to exaggerate the linking sounds as they practice and to draw a linking symbol (curved line) in the air as they say the linking /**m**/ sound.

Unit 5 Quiz is available on page 76.

Weak Syllables
Linking Vowels

Can I help you?
Yes, I'd like a pizza.

Unit overview

This unit begins by focusing on *schwa* – the weak, or reduced, *vowel sound*. This sound is at the center of a weak English *syllable*, and is perhaps the greatest barrier to English learners' listening comprehension. That is because the schwa vowel sound is the opposite of clear vowel sound: it is vague, as in the second syllable of the word "sofa." Any vowel letter can be pronounced as schwa when it is in an *unstressed syllable*. (There are actually three different forms of weak vowels, but from a beginning student's point of view they all sound pretty much alike.)

Although there is no alphabet letter for schwa, it is the most common vowel sound in spoken English, because vowels tend to become schwa when they are not stressed. This is systematic in spoken English, and the *contrast* between clear and unclear sounds makes the stressed vowel extra easy to notice.

The schwa sound is relatively uncommon in world languages, so many students need practice hearing it. The focus on schwa in this lesson is intended mainly to aid listening comprehension. Incorporating the sound into spoken English is often difficult for beginning learners, but the important goal is to help them recognize it.

After practice in recognizing and saying weak and strong syllables, students listen to and practice saying vowel *linking,* as in "coffee and milk." This leads to tasks in which students practice saying the commonly reduced words "and," "of," and "a."

Finally, students integrate the skills practiced in this unit in a restaurant conversation.

A Vowels in strong and weak syllables

To introduce the concept of the weak syllable to students, call their attention to the illustrations in the box. The three figures in the box represent strong (stressed), regular, and weak vowel sounds.

B Rules for strong and weak syllables
Class CD 2, Track 2

Go over the rules on pages 38 and 39 of the Student's Book with students. It may be useful to give students rubber bands to illustrate vowel length, as suggested in Unit 5.

> **Teaching tip**   Write these three example words on the board in big letters:
>
> *ketchup*   *mustard*   *vanilla*
>
> Underneath, rewrite each word, spelling the words with schwa:
>
> *ketchəp*   *mustərd*   *vənillə*
>
> Ask students to do the same thing with three words they choose.
>
> A quite different approach is to have students write each syllable of a three-syllable word on a separate piece of paper. For example:
>
> | *com* | *pu* | *ter* |
> | --- | --- | --- |
> | *to* | *ma* | *to* |
> | *va* | *nill* | *a* |
> | *al* | *pha* | *bet* |
>
> Choose three outgoing students to play the parts of the strong, regular, and weak vowel figures. (Remind the students of the three figures in Task A.) Have them each hold up their syllable in order, saying their syllable as they act it. If they can coordinate the syllables and the actions smoothly, they will be saying the word smoothly. This can be quite a challenge to do without laughing.

C Which vowel sounds are weak?
Class CD 2, Track 3

Tell students that in Unit 5 they listened for the strong syllable in some of these words, and now they are going to listen for the weak syllables. Have them look at the example done for them in item 1 before you play the audio or read the script, to be sure they understand what to do. After students listen, have them put the answers on the board, and check the answers with the whole class.

D Saying strong and weak syllables
Class CD 2, Track 4

Students may have very different pronunciations of (or even different words for) these country names in their own languages. As they listen to and repeat the names, students can practice with rubber bands or gestures to reinforce the pronunciations.

E Strong and weak syllables in food names
Class CD 2, Track 5

Play the audio or read the list out loud to the students. They should repeat each word at least two times.

F Linking vowels
Class CD 2, Track 6

In earlier units, students practiced linking with /n/ and /m/. Tell them that vowels can also link to each other.

Practice in linking these vowels helps learners realize why some combinations of words sound like one word (e.g., "vanilla ice" sounds like /vəˈnɪl•ə•ɑʸs/).

G Weak "and"
Class CD 2, Track 7

Tell students that it is not only syllables that can be weak – whole words can be weak, too. After students listen to the audio and repeat the phrases, encourage them to think of other examples with "and" that they may have heard, such as "fish 'n' chips," "snow 'n' ice," "dogs 'n' cats," "hot 'n' cold," "boys 'n' girls."

H Weak "and," "of," and "a"
Class CD 2, Track 8

Have students listen to the phrases on the audio and repeat them at least two times.

Note: Students might notice that the word "soup" /suʷp/ also is an exception to the vowel rules. Remind students that, although there are exceptions, the vowel rules usually work.

I Review: The One Vowel Rule
Class CD 2, Track 9

Review the One Vowel Rule with students. Before they listen to the audio, remind them to notice the weak sounds.

J Music of English
Class CD 2, Track 10

The exclamation point can give students a chance to express enthusiasm, by using their hands to show how big an "elephant-size" pizza would be. The hand gesture should occur at the first syllable of "elephant" so that the physical display matches the lengthened vowel, which is at the peak of meaning. An alternative is to have students move their heads to match the pitch lines of these sentences. This can be a slight movement or a big, comical one, but the point is that, in English, *gestural emphasis* goes with voice emphasis.

Gestures are culturally fixed and may be transferred into a second language situation. On the other hand, when learners are feeling tense in a new language, they often speak in a monotone and without any physical movement. In English, gestures need to co-occur with spoken emphasis, in order to make that emphasis quite clear. This can be demonstrated by showing a brief section of a video of a TV comedy or a speech. The same short section should be shown several times, both with and without sound, so that students can see how gesture is systematically matched with speech. One way to describe this is that "the dance always goes with the music."

Students can be helped to mark the important emphasis points by practicing some kind of gesture with their hands, or some facial gesture, such as raising their eyebrows at the point of emphasis (the *peak vowel*). This may seem funny at first, especially for students coming from cultures that tend to use only very subtle facial gestures to show emphasis or opinion (e.g., many Asian cultures).

For students from such a background, it may be important to point out that gesture is not only used to make the emphasis clear to the listener, but also to show that a listener is actually listening. It is a form of visual feedback. Usually there will be a nod, raising of eyebrows, some little noise, or some other response to show attentiveness, if not actual agreement. A face that shows no response to what the other person is saying in English usually signals disagreement or perhaps even anger. This physical responsiveness, or lack of, is another point students can watch for in a silent section of video.

Note: After students listen to the audio and repeat the sentences, have them repeat the exchange at least once more as a whole piece, to show how the meanings and intonation patterns of the sentences are linked.

K The Elephant Eatery
Class CD 2, Track 11

Have students look at the menu while they listen to the audio and repeat the words. When they finish, you can ask them if they have tried any of the foods listed on the menu. You can also ask them what items on the menu sound good or strange to them.

Note: "Iced tea" is pronounced the same as "ice tea" /ɑʸs 'tiʸ/, and it is sometimes spelled that way on menus.

"Artichokes" /'ɑrt•ə•tʃoʷks/ is not a common word, but it was chosen to show students that they can now figure out the pronunciation of an unfamiliar word, syllable by syllable. There is a drawing of an artichoke on the menu, but you might also want to tell students that it is a green vegetable composed of hard leaves, with a sharp thorn at the tip of each leaf and a soft, edible part at the base. In the United States, the center, or heart, of the artichoke is popular in salads and sometimes as a topping for pizza.

L Pair work: In the Elephant Eatery
Class CD 2, Track 12

Have students listen to the conversation on the audio and then practice it with a partner. Encourage them to overact and use gestures. If they think of it as a comedy, they will tend to feel freer to use emphasis. Choose one or two student pairs to perform the conversation for the class.

M Pair work: Ordering food

Encourage students to use gestures, as they did in Task L. If they are able, students can add menu items to make this role play more fun (e.g., "spaghetti," "steak," "fruit salad," etc.). When they finish, choose one or two pairs to perform their conversations for the class.

N Food game

Put students into groups of four or five, and have them make a list of food words. The food names should have two or more syllables. Make the game more interesting by awarding points separately for correctly identifying the number of syllables and for underlining the strong syllable.

Students may think of food names in which both syllables have roughly equal strength, and which are therefore worth two points, for the underlined syllables (e.g., "beefsteak," "pancakes," "meatloaf"). Other foods to suggest if students get stuck are:

tuna	/'tuʷ•nə/
apples	/'æp•əlz/
peaches	/'piʸ•tʃəz/
mustard	/'mʌs•tərd/
vinegar	/'vɪn•ɪ•gər/
cookies	/'kʊk•iʸz/
pudding	/'pʊd•ɪŋ/
muffin	/'mʌf•ən/
lettuce	/'lɛt•əs/
crackers	/'kræk•ərz/
omelet	/'ɑm•lət/
asparagus	/ə'spær•ə•gəs/
spaghetti	/spə'gɛt•iʸ/

Note: Nouns are usually stressed on the first syllable, but not always (e.g., "spaghetti" and "asparagus").

O Review: Strong syllables

In this task, students simply fill in the strong (stressed) syllable after they have looked at the word and the symbol for the vowel sound of the stressed syllable (the peak vowel). This exercise should help students focus on the central importance of the peak vowel in the strong syllable.

Answer Key
1. lem
2. sand
3. chick

Unit 6 Quiz is available on page 77.

7 The Most Important Word

Are you going to eat dinner at nine?
No, at six.

Unit overview

In Unit 7, students build on what they have learned about *strong* and *weak syllables* by focusing on word *emphasis* in sentences. In English, emphasis is mainly signaled by intonation, with a large *pitch change* on the *most important word*, the focus of the sentence or *word group*. This pitch change occurs on the primary stressed syllable (strong syllable) and that is exactly where the vowel must be extra long and extra clear. This is the *peak vowel* in the word group. Other languages use different means to make clear which word is most important: perhaps word order, or a special particle or word that alerts the listener to notice a certain part of a message. Language-specific systems for emphasis are learned so early that they are applied unconsciously to any new language, so it is necessary to train students to notice the English way of using length difference and the change of pitch on the peak vowel of the primary stress (strong syllable) of the most important word.

In this unit, students practice specific communication skills connected with word emphasis: pointing out and clarifying misunderstandings, and correcting mistakes about the date and time.

A The most important thing

Call students' attention to the two pictures of the rabbit, and ask, "What makes the rabbit easy to see?" If students need help, the answer to this question is in the box just beneath the pictures. These graphic images are meant to convey the importance of intonation.

B The most important word
Class CD 2, Track 13

1. The box labeled "Easy to hear" is meant to teach students that the pitch change, the lengthening of the primary stress and the weakening or reducing of many of the vowels are a systematic way to highlight the most important word (or focus word) of a word group (sentence, clause, or phrase). Linking ties the words in a word group together, making a rhythmic context in which the most important word can easily be identified by the listener. In fact, there is often little real lengthening for the stressed syllable of any word unless it is the focus of a word group.

2. Play the audio or read the sentences out loud. Encourage students to trace the pitch lines in the Student's Book as they listen, to help them feel how the pitch changes on the focus word in each sentence.

3. Go over the rules for the most important word. In some languages, the most important word is automatically placed at a particular position in the sentence. But since this word can be anywhere in an English sentence, the intonational marking is crucial.

It is not so important in which direction the voice changes pitch. What really matters is that there is a change either up or down from the baseline pitch. This calls the listener's attention to the focus word. Students often go up or down on many words, hoping this will make them more intelligible. But this is as damaging to the English system of intonational marking as is speaking in a monotone. English has very little grammatical or other means to call attention to the most important word, so the pitch change is an essential signal of importance or focus.

Note: If a word is said alone, it is a complete utterance and, therefore, the word will have the lengthening and pitch change of a word group. That means that "electrification" will have the same musical pattern as "We went to the station."

C Music of English
Class CD 2, Track 14

After students listen to the audio and repeat the sentences, have them repeat the exchange at least once more as a whole piece, to show how the meanings and intonation patterns of the sentences are linked. Do not rush this kind of practice. If it is done thoroughly, it can give students confidence in marrying the music to the words.

Teaching tip A kazoo (a toy humming instrument) is an excellent tool for helping students pay attention to the change of pitch. The kazoo amplifies the *vibration* in the *vocal cords* and thus conveys the *pitch pattern* of the voice without the distraction of individual sounds. You can use a kazoo to demonstrate the pitch pattern, but it is also a powerful tool if each student can have a kazoo to practice with. You may be able to buy kazoos at a party supply store but, if they are not available where you live, you can simply "sing" the pitch pattern with an "ahhhh" sound. Students should practice this in chorus, until everyone is singing the melody of the sentence together accurately. Then they will be ready to practice this with the words.

Note: If you blow into the kazoo, there will be no sound. You must hum in order for the vibration of the vocal cords to be amplified. If you blow, there will be no vibration and therefore no sound to amplify.

D Pair work: The most important word
Class CD 2, Track 15

Ask the students to pay attention to the intonation of the highlighted words as they listen to the conversations.

E Pair work: Finding the most important word

Now students must decide which word is most important. They should follow the model in Task D. If students have enough vocabulary, they can supply words of their own to these dialogues about losing things. Choose one or two pairs to perform their conversations for the class.

Answer Key

1. **The Shoes**
   Jean: What's <u>wrong</u>?
   Joan: I lost my <u>shoes</u>.
   Jean: <u>Which</u> shoes?
   Joan: My <u>tennis</u> shoes.
2. **The Dog**
   Jim: What's the <u>problem</u>?
   Mike: I lost my <u>dog</u>.
   Jim: What <u>kind</u> of dog?
   Mike: A <u>brown</u> dog. A small brown <u>dog</u>.
   Jim: I <u>saw</u> a small brown dog. It was at the <u>supermarket</u>.

3. **A Letter**
   Bob: What are you <u>doing</u>?
   Jenny: I'm writing a <u>letter</u>.
   Bob: What <u>kind</u> of letter?
   Jenny: A <u>business</u> letter.
   Bob: What <u>kind</u> of business?
   Jenny: <u>Personal</u> business!

F Music of English
Class CD 2, Track 16

This "music box" introduces the useful skill of polite disagreement. It also gives students an opportunity to work on word order and the plural / singular distinction for auxiliary verbs in short answers.

It seems illogical to some learners to emphasize "are" and "is" in the negative *contractions* "aren't," and "isn't." But this is the way native English speakers speak these words, and it is important for students to learn to recognize the actual negative meaning.

Teaching tip A challenging and entertaining way to encourage a physical sense of the music in these sentences is through the game of "Syllablettes," developed by William Acton. In this game, teams plan how to demonstrate a sentence of up to six or seven syllables (e.g., "When are we going?"), building on the word practice suggested in the beginning of Unit 6, Task B. Each student represents one syllable and must show their form as strong, regular, or weak. Adventurous teams could add in linking and variable pitch height. Then they should practice saying their syllables in sequence while physically demonstrating the degree of syllable strength, producing the sentence in a smooth, continuous flow.

G Pair work: Disagreement

You can introduce this task by making some obviously incorrect statements to the class. For example:

This is a Spanish class.
Today is very hot / cold. (Say the opposite of the truth.)
This is a dog. (Hold up a book.)

Students may be surprised by this at first, but you can shake your head no, and encourage them to disagree with you. Then have students underline the most important word in each word group and say the conversations two times with a partner. They should switch roles the second time.

Because it is important for students to recognize which is the crucial word in the disagreements, this exercise should be practiced several times. To make it more interesting and useful, have students practice with different partners.

Note: It may be helpful to pre-teach the pronunciation of some of the vocabulary, such as "Ottawa" /ˈɑ•tə•wə/.

Answer Key

1. A: California is a <u>city</u>.
   B: <u>No</u>, it <u>isn't</u>. It's a <u>state</u>.
2. A: Ice is <u>hot</u>.
   B: <u>No</u>, it <u>isn't</u>. It's <u>cold</u>.
3. A: Lemons are <u>sweet</u>.
   B: <u>No</u>, they <u>aren't</u>. <u>Honey</u> is sweet.
4. A: Babies are <u>bigger</u> than children.
   B: <u>No</u>, they <u>aren't</u>. They're <u>smaller</u> than children.
5. A: Fish eat <u>grass</u>.
   B: <u>No</u>, they <u>don't</u>. They eat <u>smaller</u> fish.
6. A: The world is <u>flat</u>.
   B: <u>No</u>, it <u>isn't</u>. It's <u>round</u>.
7. A: You buy books at a <u>library</u>.
   B: <u>No</u>, you <u>don't</u>. You buy books at a <u>bookstore</u>.
8. A: You borrow books at a <u>bookstore</u>.
   B: <u>No</u>, you <u>don't</u>. You borrow books at a <u>library</u>.
9. A: Cars travel in the <u>air</u>.
   B: <u>No</u>, they <u>don't</u>. They travel on the <u>road</u>.
10. A: <u>Toronto</u> is the capital of Canada.
    B: <u>No</u>, it <u>isn't</u>. <u>Ottawa</u> is the capital of Canada.

H Music of English
Class CD 2, Track 17

In certain cultures, people will not usually point out misunderstandings if they are served the wrong item at a restaurant. Tell students that in many English-speaking cultures it is all right to do so. This exercise will give them the intonation to point out misunderstandings clearly and politely.

I Pair work: Misunderstandings

After reading the directions, model the task by taking the part of Student A and choosing someone in the class to take the part of Student B. Then put students into pairs, and have them take turns correcting and responding to the misunderstandings. Remind students to choose sentence **a** or **b** at random, to keep the exercise interesting. If students have enough vocabulary, they can develop some of their own misunderstandings and then share them with the class.

J Music of English
Class CD 2, Track 18

You could demonstrate how exaggerating the intonation even more makes the questioner sound surprised or shocked.

K Pair work: Correcting a mistake about time

In this exercise, students practice a useful social skill: correcting mistakes or misunderstandings about time. This will be especially helpful when they need to make appointments or reservations in English.

L Review: Counting syllables
Class CD 2, Track 19

After students listen to the days of the week and write the number of syllables, have them practice saying the days out loud. This will prepare them for the next task, in which they correct mistakes about the days of the week.

Answer Key

1. Monday   2
2. Tuesday   2
3. Wednesday   2
4. Thursday   2
5. Friday   2
6. Saturday   3
7. Sunday   2

M Pair work: Correcting a mistake about the day

This exercise is similar to Task K, but students correct information about days rather than times. Note that the sentences in this unit are longer, and the grammar is more complicated than in previous units. The length of the sentence (e.g., "Are you going to see the doctor on Monday?") makes it harder for the student to decide which part of the sentence is most important to highlight. This is a good time to point out that there can be more than one word group in a sentence, and therefore more than one most important word (and more than one peak vowel).

Teaching tip If students have enough language, this can be made into an information gap exercise. Make copies of a blank page of a weekly appointment book for students. Put students into pairs, and have partners ask each other if they plan to do something at a particular hour or day of the week. They then can fill in each other's schedules. The main thing to practice is *emphasizing* the important information and correcting the misinformation. When the speaker successfully emphasizes a particular word (the hour or the day of the week), it is like shining a flashlight beam on the exact information desired.

N Review: Most important words

In this task students are asked to think about which word in the sentence is important. The purpose is to help students connect this word to the most important syllable (e.g., the strong syllable *Sat-*) and the peak vowel /æ/. The peak vowel is the peak of information and helps the listener recognize the most important word.

> ### Answer Key
>
> 1. Sunday
> 2. Saturday

Unit 7 Quiz is available on page 78.

8 Stop Sounds /t/ and /d/ and Continuing Sounds /s/ and /z/ Linking with /t/, /d/, /s/, and /z/ Sounds

How do you spell "fruit"?
Is she running? No, she's reading.

Unit overview

Unit 8 introduces the contrasting concepts of *stop sounds and continuing sounds* (or continuants), using the pairs /**t**/ or /**d**/ and /**s**/ or /**z**/.

The final sounds /**s**/ and /**z**/ are particularly important in English because they mark plural nouns, third-person singular verbs, and possessives (e.g., "books," "he runs," and "Jack's book"). *Clear Speech From the Start* concentrates on the distinction between singular and plural, because it is so important for clear communication.

The continuing sounds /**s**/ and /**z**/ are distinguished only by the presence or absence of *vibration*, or *voicing*, in the *vocal cords*. That is, the final sound in "bus," /**s**/, is *voiceless*, and the final sound in "buzz," /**z**/, is *voiced*. The same is true for /**t**/ and /**d**/; they are alike in every way except for voicing. Since the voiced / voiceless distinction is not a high priority for students at this stage of learning, it is not presented in *Clear Speech From the Start* in order to keep the tasks simple for the students and to allow them to concentrate on the stop / continuing sound distinction.

A Stop sounds and continuing sounds
Class CD 2, Track 20

1. Call students' attention to the diagrams on page 54 of the Student's Book. Unlike traditional side view drawings, these illustrations aim to show how changes in the way the air flows through the mouth create stops and continuing sounds. To make the stop sounds /**t**/ or /**d**/, the tongue blocks airflow out of the mouth by pressing against the tooth ridge all the way around the front of the mouth. To make the continuing sounds /**s**/ or /**z**/, air is forced through a narrow V-shaped passage at high pressure. The friction (or *turbulence*) created by the flow of air through this narrow passage is the cause of the characteristic hissing associated with *sibilant* sounds. It also is what distinguishes these sounds from /**θ**/ or /**ð**/ (e.g., "**th**anks" / "**th**is"), which have no turbulence because the tongue is flat for both of these sounds. These sounds will be introduced in Unit 15. See the drawings comparing /**s**/, /**θ**/, and /**t**/ on page 109 of the Student's Book.

To demonstrate the difference between a stop and a continuing sound, walk around the room saying "bus," continuing the /**s**/ until you run out of air. Then say "but," throwing up the palm of your hand, facing the class, in a "stop" gesture, at the end of the word. Don't release any air after the /**t**/ sound; just stop. Another way to show the contrast: move your hand across the space in front of you to represent a continuing sound as you say "bus," and then make the stop gesture with the hand when you say "but." These hand signals match the stop sign and arrow shown in the task, and they can also be used by students, to help them concentrate on the stop / continuing sound distinction.

The difference between a stop and a continuing sound is most apparent at the end of a word, so that is the position where it is easiest to demonstrate. However, a more important reason to concentrate only on the ends of words is that this is where consonants can function as grammatical signals, e.g., "book" / "books," "can" / "can't," "I go" / "I'd go."

Allow students to try out the feel of these sounds for themselves quietly while they look at the mouth pictures. Time given to this physical introspection and experimentation is not the same as asking students to listen and repeat words. It gives students a personal orientation to the airflow requirements of the two sounds. Therefore, in the next few tasks, students should *not* repeat the words they hear, but they should concentrate only on listening.

Note: The stop sounds in English are /**p**/, /**b**/, /**t**/, /**d**/, /**k**/, and /**g**/, plus the *combination sounds* (*affricates*) /**tʃ**/ and /**dʒ**/, as in the first and last sounds in "**ch**ur**ch**" and "**j**u**dg**e." All the other sounds, including vowels, are continuants.

2. In this exercise, students just listen and should not try to repeat the words. Repeating out loud what they have just heard will tend to obscure the acoustic imprint in their minds. They should be encouraged to be patient and just listen at this stage.

🎧 B Which word do you hear?
Class CD 2, Track 21

Have students circle the words they hear. When checking answers, you might want to have students tell you whether the final sounds stop or continue.

Audio Script

1.	bus	/bʌs/
2.	tickets	/ˈtɪk•əts/
3.	beds	/bɛdz/
4.	is	/ɪz/
5.	white	/waʸt/
6.	nice	/naʸs/
7.	right	/raʸt/
8.	has	/hæz/

Answer Key

1. but (bus)
2. ticket (tickets)
3. bed (beds)
4. it (is)
5. (white) wise
6. night (nice)
7. (right) rice
8. had (has)

🎧 C Which word is different?
Class CD 2, Track 22

Have students listen and check the different word. Do not worry about the difference between /**d**/ and /**t**/ or /**s**/ and /**z**/. Only ask students to notice whether the final sound is a stop or a continuing sound.

Write the answers on the board, or have the students say the letters of the correct answers in unison.

Audio Script

1. right, right, rice
   /raʸt/, /raʸt/, /raʸs/
2. bus, bus, but
   /bʌs/, /bʌs/, /bʌt/

3. white, wise, wise
   /waʸt/, /waʸz/, /waʸz/
4. beds, bed, bed
   /bɛdz/, /bɛd/, /bɛd/
5. night, night, nice
   /naʸt/, /naʸt/, /naʸs/
6. boat, boats, boat
   /boʷt/, /boʷts/, /boʷt/
7. flight, flies, flight
   /flaʸt/, /flaʸz/, /flaʸt/
8. hat, hat, hats
   /hæt/, /hæt/, /hæts/

Answer Key

	X	Y	Z
1.			✓
2.			✓
3.	✓		
4.	✓		
5.			✓
6.		✓	
7.		✓	
8.			✓

🎧 D Final sounds: Stop or continue?
Class CD 2, Track 23

Make sure students cover the words the first time they listen to this exercise. They should be relying on their ears rather than on the spelling.

Answer Key

		STOP	➡
1. bus	1.		✓
2. but	2.	✓	
3. rice	3.		✓
4. seats	4.		✓
5. had	5.	✓	
6. boat	6.	✓	
7. cheese	7.		✓
8. ride	8.	✓	
9. cakes	9.		✓
10. night	10.	✓	

E Pair work: Is it one or more than one?

This task introduces the grammatical significance of the final sibilant sound, /s/ or /z/. The spelling is often misleading, so it is important that students learn to use their ears, not rely on their eyes. Go over the instructions and examples with your students. It can be useful to give some additional examples and have students respond in unison before they begin the pair work. Remind them to choose **a** or **b** words at random to keep the activity challenging. Depending on the level of the class, it may be appropriate to teach students the terms "singular" and "plural."

If possible, have students change partners two or three times. If students all belong to the same first-language group, this kind of pair work may not work as well as in a multilingual class, because the students may use non-English cues to signal a difficult sound (e.g., extra tension in their voice or body for the sound students know is extra difficult). Even in this situation, the practice is useful because it helps focus on the final consonant and the fact that it makes a difference to meaning.

F Music of English
Class CD 2, Track 24

Many kinds of active responses can also reinforce emphasis. Have students rise up a bit from their seats as they emphasize the important syllable, or bow a bit from the waist or raise their eyebrows (this takes more concentration than it sounds). Physical marking of the important syllable can bring major improvement in intelligibility.

G Pair work: How do you spell "hats"?

After reading the directions, ask students to read the examples. Then model the task by taking the part of Student A and choosing someone in the class to take the part of Student B. Act out choosing a question to ask, then have Student B answer your question. Confirm or correct the answer. Then put students into pairs. You could give the class some additional examples and have them answer in unison before they start the pair work.

Note: "Repeats" (in item 8) is more likely to be used as a third-person singular verb rather than a plural noun. This grammatical construction is harder to learn than the plural and is introduced here only so that students become used to hearing the sound of a final /s/. When they study the third-person singular, this familiarity with the sound will help.

> **Teaching tip** To help students say the consonant cluster /d/ or /t/ plus /s/, have them practice linking these phrases:
> had six
> white socks

H Linking with /t/ and /d/
Class CD 2, Track 25

Some students might want to practice the difference between /t/ and /d/ at this stage. Tell them not to worry about this now and to concentrate on the distinction between the stop / continuant sounds. If necessary, assure the students that the tongue is in the same position when producing both /t/ and /d/. The only difference is in the presence or absence of voicing, which means the vibration of the vocal cords, and this is not presented until the higher-level book, *Clear Speech*, because tongue placement is enough of a challenge at the lower level.

> **Teaching tip** Linking exercises can be done with the whole class or in pairs. Students may be helped to focus on this linking by bringing their hands together as they speak when two sounds are to be linked. Some people find that this helps them concentrate, while others find it distracting. Give students an opportunity to experiment.

I Linking with /s/ and /z/
Class CD 2, Track 26

Go over the instructions with students before they listen to the audio. Examples of /s/ or /z/ sounds linking to another continuing sound, rather than simply to a vowel, occur in step 2, sentences 2 ("Gus said"), 5 ("It's so"), 6 ("is new"), 7 ("She's never"), and 8 ("His mother"). If students are advanced enough, have them find these examples for you.

J Review: The Two Vowel Rule
Class CD 2, Track 27

This review of vowel sounds includes words that end in stopping or continuing consonants, so that students will have to think about two things at once. Review the rule in the box with students.

On the audio, the students will hear the words read downward, in columns. If you feel they need more of a challenge, have them say the words across, in rows.

K Music of English
Class CD 2, Track 28

Students often emphasize a pronoun, even when it is not the main point. This may be because of a rule in their native language, but it is likely to confuse a native English-speaking listener, since pronouns are emphasized in English only when they are specifically meant to be the focus of attention. While the main point of this particular task is the reduction of the pronoun, it is also useful to point out that the word "is" is linked to the following pronoun, "she" or "he."

L Pair work: Correcting a mistake
Class CD 2, Track 29

In this exercise, students review what they learned in Unit 7 about how to correct mistakes and add the concept of linking continuants to following pronouns.

Have students listen to and repeat the names of the activities in step 1. A useful approach is to point to or have students point to the pictures of activities in the box on page 61 of the Student's Book as they listen. Then go over the instructions and example with students before having them do the pair work. If they have enough language, they can ask questions about activities other than those listed in step 1.

M S-Ball game

This extra task is a challenging game because it introduces the third person singular, which is a difficult grammatical lesson to learn. It also requires students to practice saying words ending in the letters -**er**, /ər/, which is difficult for many learners. But if your students are lively (or need to get up and do something lively), this game can capture their attention.

To play this game, you will need to bring to class several small, lightweight balls – one for each group of four or five students. If no balls are readily available, you can have students crumple a sheet of paper into a ball. After reading the instructions, model the example with three students. Then put students into groups of four or five, and have them play the game.

Don't let the Leader ask these questions in sequence (1, 2, 3, etc.) because that makes the game too easy. Accept either an /**s**/ or a /**z**/ sound for all these word endings. Both sibilants mean "third person singular." Leave the voicing distinction for later teaching. The faster the game, the more fun, assuming the class is advanced enough to take the pressure.

Unit 8 Quiz is available on page 79.

9 Final Sounds /d/ and /l/ Linking with /l/

How do you spell "whale"?
What does "paid" mean?

Unit overview

Like Unit 8, this unit focuses on the distinction between word-final *stops* and *continuants*, this time with /**d**/ and /**l**/. This leads to tasks in which students practice hearing and producing the final /**l**/ in the *contracted* form of "will" (as in "I'll").

In many ESL/EFL pronunciation courses, primary attention is given to contrasting the sounds /**r**/ and /**l**/, as students from many language backgrounds have difficulty distinguishing these sounds. However, since many students have already experienced frustration trying to hear or make this distinction, it can be helpful instead to contrast these sounds with different sounds, giving students a new perspective. In Unit 11, /**r**/ is compared with the now familiar /**d**/.

A Final sounds /d/ and /l/
Class CD 2, Track 30

It is important to give students enough time to think about the pictures on page 63 of the Student's Book and to try to feel the sound in their own mouths. They may find it helpful to look at the pictures of the tongue shapes for several sounds in Appendix D on pages 134 and 135 of the Student's Book. After students have looked at the pictures, draw their attention to the arrows indicating the airflow at the front of the mouth for the sound /**l**/. The back of the tongue is low, allowing air to continue to flow through these openings at either side of the tip of the tongue.

English learners will have an easier time making this sound clearly if they touch the tooth ridge (the "alveolar ridge," which is the horseshoe-shaped bump inside the mouth) for both initial and final /**l**/.

B Which word do you hear?
Class CD 2, Track 31

To help students overcome interference between the letters and the sounds, it can be useful to ask them to listen without reading (covering up the print) and to say (or write) whether they think the word ends or "continues." Then ask students to listen again and check their answers. Alternatively, they could draw a stop sign or an arrow, which are again being used to represent the concepts of stop sound and continuing sound.

Audio Script

1. made /meʸd/
2. fool /fuʷl/
3. roll /roʷl/
4. bed /bɛd/
5. paid /peʸd/
6. tile /tɑʸl/
7. fade /feʸd/
8. feel /fiʸl/

Answer Key

1. (made) mail
2. food (fool)
3. road (roll)
4. (bed) bell
5. (paid) pale
6. tide (tile)
7. (fade) fail
8. feed (feel)

Teaching tip Another way to help focus attention on the final sounds /**d**/ and /**l**/ is to make lists of words that end in these sounds, with the letters -**d**- and -**l**- written in color. Use red for -**d**- because the word "red" ends in a final /**d**/ sound; use purple for -**l**- because the word "purple" ends in an /**l**/ sound. Write the words "red" and "purple" on the board, with the -**d**- in red and the -**l**- in purple. Then have students suggest other words with final /**d**/ and /**l**/ sounds to go below these key words. Include any word with a final /**d**/ or /**l**/ sound, even if it is spelled with a silent letter -**e**- at the end (as in "purple"). Students can make their own charts, using a red or purple marker when they get to the final letter.

This kinesthetic activity helps students focus on these two final sounds. This is especially helpful for students from languages that tend not to have final consonants.

To give students a chance to work in a more active mode, you might ask them to listen to each word and say "stop" or "continue." Or, they could hold up a hand for "stop," or draw a continuing line in the air for "continue."

C Which word is different?
Class CD 2, Track 32

Audio Script

1. food, food, fool
   /fuʷd/, /fuʷd/, /fuʷl/
2. bell, bed, bed
   /bɛl/, /bɛd/, /bɛd/
3. tile, tile, tide
   /taʸl/, /taʸl/, /taʸd/
4. road, road, roll
   /roʷd/, /roʷd/, /roʷl/
5. paid, pail, paid
   /peʸd/, /peʸl/, /peʸd/
6. made, made, mail
   /meʸd/, /meʸd/, /meʸl/
7. seed, seal, seal
   /siʸd/, /siʸl/, /siʸl/
8. feed, feed, feel
   /fiʸd/, /fiʸd/, /fiʸl/

Answer Key

	X	Y	Z
1.			✓
2.	✓		
3.			✓
4.			✓
5.		✓	
6.			✓
7.	✓		
8.			✓

D Saying final sounds /d/ and /l/
Class CD 2, Track 33

It is helpful to have students practice **whispering** these words before they say them out loud. Whispering helps students establish an acoustic image of the sounds they are trying to produce, which is an important step in the process of learning to articulate new sounds. Whispering also changes the atmosphere in a class and can make the task more intriguing. Demonstrate whispering, and let students experiment for a bit before doing the full exercise.

E Music of English
Class CD 2, Track 34

This task is meant to help students put final /**d**/ and /**l**/ into a proper rhythmic context.

F Pair work: Hearing and saying final /d/ and /l/

Some of these words may be unfamiliar, which makes them good practice material for these useful questions. Before beginning, point to each picture, and have students repeat the words ("mail," "roll," "bed," "bell," "whale," "wade," "feed," "pail"). After pair practice, work as a class, and ask individual students the questions.

Teaching tip Give students a homework assignment to listen for two words, one ending in /**d**/ and one ending in /**l**/. Asking for only two words makes this an easy assignment, but it will encourage students to start paying attention outside of class. They can bring these words to the next class and add them to a color-coded list. (See Teaching tip for Task B above.) Any activity that makes students focus on these final sounds will be of special help to students who tend to drop final consonants.

G Listening for final /l/: Present or future?
Class CD 2, Track 35

This is meant not as a grammar lesson but instead to increase students' awareness that the final /l/ sound can make a difference in meaning by signaling future tense.

"Going to" as a form of the future was reviewed in Unit 7, Tasks J, K, and M. "Will," and especially the final /l/, which is a contracted / reduced form of this word for future tense, is harder to hear. Therefore, it is important to listen for this sound, to improve listening comprehension.

Answer Key

1. a. I read the newspaper. — Present
   b. I'll read the newspaper. — (Future)
2. a. I drink coffee. — Present
   b. I'll drink coffee. — (Future)
3. a. I drive to work. — (Present)
   b. I'll drive to work. — Future
4. a. I take the train. — Present
   b. I'll take the train. — (Future)
5. a. We ride the bus. — Present
   b. We'll ride the bus. — (Future)
6. a. They go home. — (Present)
   b. They'll go home. — Future
7. a. We watch TV. — (Present)
   b. We'll watch TV. — Future
8. a. They go to the movies. — Present
   b. They'll go to the movies. — (Future)

H Pair work: Present or future?
Class CD 2, Track 36

As with previous pair work tasks, go over the examples with the class before they practice in pairs. After the pair work, gather the class together and have individual students read and respond to the statements.

If students are ready for more of a challenge, have them use other expressions of time (e.g., "next Friday," "each morning," "after this week," etc.). Write these expressions on the board. To model, have students read different sentences from the task, and respond yourself using the new expressions on the board. Then have students practice in pairs.

I Linking with /l/
Class CD 2, Track 37

It helps some students to link (touch) their fingers together while saying the linking sound. Physical gestures can be powerful reminders of abstract concepts.

J Review: Counting syllables in sentences
Class CD 2, Track 38

Syllable number should be reviewed often, as it needs repeated reinforcement. Awareness of syllables is essential for correct rhythm, and it can also have an important effect on the grammatical accuracy of students' speech and writing. Students who have not learned to attend to the number of syllables in an utterance are more likely to miss the small structure words (e.g., prepositions, auxiliary verbs, articles, etc.) that are pronounced less clearly in natural spoken English. These students will tend to leave these important words out of their own speech and writing as well.

Answer Key

1. Make a bowl of rice. — 1. 5
2. We need two plates. — 2. 4
3. They like ice cubes. — 3. 4
4. Joe needed five tickets. — 4. 6
5. We cleaned the plates. — 5. 4

Unit 9 Quiz is available on page 80.

10 Final Sounds /l/ and /ld/
Linking with All the Stop Sounds

Did you say "coal"?
No, I said "cold."

Unit overview

In this unit, learners focus on the distinction between the word-final sounds /l/ and /ld/, particularly when they occur in verbs, where the distinction can signal the difference between present and past tense. Students also practice confirming whether the word they heard was correct and *linking* the English *stop sounds,* /t/, /d/, /p/, /b/, /k/, and /g/, to vowels at the beginning of the next word.

A Final sounds /l/ and /ld/
Class CD 2, Track 39

As students listen to the audio, remind them not to repeat the words. If they are really anxious to speak, ask them to *whisper* only, so that they do not confuse their own pronunciation with the accurate model. This is one of the most important reasons to encourage students to listen without repeating during the early learning of a new sound.

Note: Help students notice that these are all one-syllable words. This activity reminds them to use their ears to determine the number of *syllables*, rather than depending on their eyes.

> **Teaching tip** Another approach is to ask students to circle each word as they hear it. Or you could have them make the hand gestures for "stop" and "continue."

B Present and past
Class CD 2, Track 40

Here students listen to determine whether the sentences they hear are in the present or past tense, by focusing on the final /l/ and /ld/ sounds. Give students a minute or two to read the sentences. Then have them cover the sentences with their hands or a piece of paper as they listen and mark the sentences present or past. Then have them listen again while looking at the sentences.

Answer Key

		Present	Past
1. I called a friend.	1.		✓
2. I sail a boat on Sundays.	2.	✓	
3. We mail a letter every day.	3.	✓	
4. We mailed everything.	4.		✓
5. We fill our glasses.	5.	✓	
6. A cow made our milk.	6.		✓
7. We sealed all the letters.	7.		✓

C Pair work: What does "mail" mean?

Here students ask each other questions to test how clearly they distinguish between the final /l/ and /ld/ sounds.

Go over the instructions and examples with students. Use the illustrations provided to help them understand new vocabulary. Tell them not to worry if there are still other words they don't know in this task. Some of the vocabulary may be unfamiliar, but that makes this task extra useful.

Remind students to choose questions **a** or **b** at random to keep the activity challenging.

D Pair work: Present and past
Class CD 2, Track 41

This task gives learners more practice in clearly distinguishing final /d/ and /ld/ sounds. It also introduces some useful time expressions.

Have students listen to the audio and repeat the time expressions at least two times.

Go over the instructions and examples with students before having them do the pair work.

If possible, have students change partners two or three times. If students all belong to the same first language group, this kind of pair work may not work as well as in a multilingual class because the students may use non-English cues to signal a difficult sound (e.g., extra tension in their voice or body for the sound students know is extra difficult). Even in this situation, the practice is useful because it helps focus on the final consonant and the fact that it makes a difference in meaning.

Note: The letter **-t-** is usually silent in "often" in North American English (/ˈɔ•fən/).

Teaching tip After students finish Task D, have them think of two or three words that can be substituted in each of these sentences, which you can then put on the board. (Some words will have a comical effect.) Then have the students do the task again, using these substitute words in the past / present pairs. For example:

1. I call(ed)   a doctor.
                   a taxi.
                   an elephant.

2. We fill(ed)   the box.
                   our glasses.
                   the shop with noise.

3. We sail(ed)   on the sea.
                   our toy boats.
                   in a bathtub.

4. Babies spill(ed) juice.
                     water.
                     everything.

5. The boys fail(ed) the exam.
                      to jump over the cow.
                      to win a prize.

6. They smile(d)   often.
                   at everything.
                   in a friendly way.

7. I mail(ed)   a postcard.
                   a box.
                   a refrigerator.

8. They spell(ed) everything.
                   big words.
                   their names wrong.

🎧 E Music of English
Class CD 2, Track 42

Any kind of physical movement can help fix the musical patterns needed for clarity. This can be simply a slight movement (raising hands, heads, eyebrows, etc.). You might want to remind students that, in English, gestural emphasis goes with voice emphasis. This is not true of all cultures.

Teaching tip If your students have access to TV (or news videos online) in English, suggest that they watch with the sound off, to notice how the faces of the speakers change during emphasis.

F Pair work: Did you say "made"?

Go over the instructions and examples with your students. This task asks students to pretend that they misheard a word. If doing so makes them uneasy, explain that it is an opportunity to practice verifying information when they are not sure what was just said.

🎧 G Linking stop sounds to vowels
Class CD 2, Track 43

A stop sound at the end of a word, coming before a word that begins with a vowel, "moves" to join the vowel and thus sounds like the beginning of the next word. This can make what sounds like a completely different word. For example:

"Cold ice" sounds like "coal dice."
"Paid Ann" sounds like "Pay Dan."

It can be helpful to write these examples on the board to help students exaggerate the links as they repeat them.

Unit 10 Quiz is available on page 81.

11 Final Sounds /t/, /d/, and /r/
Linking with /r/

What is it?
Where is it?

Unit overview

In this unit, learners contrast the final *stop sounds* /t/ and /d/ with the final sound /r/, a *continuing sound*. The sound /r/ is a challenging one for many students, perhaps stemming from confusion about the letter **-r-** used to represent it. In many other languages, this letter may be pronounced with a tap of the tongue on the roof of the mouth (or a flap backwards, or a trill). To a native English speaker, this kind of pronunciation can sound like a stop sound and may be misinterpreted as a /d/ (e.g., "hire" may sound like "hide"). To make the problem even more difficult, an /r/ sound often changes the vowel that comes just before it (e.g., the difference in vowel quality between "feed" and "fear"). This is one more reason to encourage students to listen specifically for the presence of a stop or continuant consonant at the end of the word.

The main feature of the sound represented by the letter **-r-** in North American English is that it is a continuing sound. For students who tend to pronounce the letter **-r-** with a stop quality, the combination of /r/ + /d/ is especially difficult and can cause a loss of the past tense grammar signal in words that end in /rd/, for example, "feared."

🎧 A Final sounds /t/, /d/, and /r/
Class CD 2, Track 44

1. Before students listen to the audio in step 2, have them look at and compare the illustrations for /t/ and /d/, and /r/. They need to notice that /r/ is a continuing sound.
2. Have students make the hand gestures for "stop" (an upraised palm of the hand) and "continue" (a moving, pointed finger) as they listen. Remind them not to repeat the words just yet. If they are really anxious to speak, ask them to *whisper* only. This silent, listening approach helps avoid the tendency to confuse the auditory image.

🎧 B Which word do you hear?
Class CD 2, Track 45

Here students listen for the distinction between final /t/ or /d/ sounds and /r/ sounds. Have them listen to the audio and circle the words they hear.

<table>
<tr><td colspan="3">Audio Script</td></tr>
<tr><td>1.</td><td>bed</td><td>/bɛd/</td></tr>
<tr><td>2.</td><td>are</td><td>/ɑr/</td></tr>
<tr><td>3.</td><td>card</td><td>/kɑrd/</td></tr>
<tr><td>4.</td><td>shared</td><td>/ʃɛrd/</td></tr>
<tr><td>5.</td><td>fire</td><td>/fɑʸr/</td></tr>
<tr><td>6.</td><td>where</td><td>/wɛr/</td></tr>
<tr><td>7.</td><td>hired</td><td>/hɑʸrd/</td></tr>
<tr><td>8.</td><td>feared</td><td>/fɪrd/</td></tr>
<tr><td>9.</td><td>poured</td><td>/poʷrd/</td></tr>
<tr><td>10.</td><td>feet</td><td>/fiʸt/</td></tr>
</table>

<table>
<tr><td colspan="2">Answer Key</td></tr>
<tr><td>1. (bed)</td><td>bear</td></tr>
<tr><td>2. art</td><td>(are)</td></tr>
<tr><td>3. (card)</td><td>car</td></tr>
<tr><td>4. (shared)</td><td>share</td></tr>
<tr><td>5. fired</td><td>(fire)</td></tr>
<tr><td>6. what</td><td>(where)</td></tr>
<tr><td>7. (hired)</td><td>hire</td></tr>
<tr><td>8. (feared)</td><td>fear</td></tr>
<tr><td>9. (poured)</td><td>pour</td></tr>
<tr><td>10. (feet)</td><td>fear</td></tr>
</table>

🎧 C Which word is different?
Class CD 2, Track 46

Here students listen for the distinction between the final sounds /t/ or /d/ and /r/.

Have them listen to the audio and put a check mark for the words that are different.

The /r/ sound can affect the vowel sound that comes before it. That is why the vowels in words like "neat" and "near" do not sound exactly the same. The vowel sound is longer in "near," because there is a slight *off-glide* to link to the final /r/. However, from the learner's point of view, the stop or continuant quality of the final consonant is the crucial distinction.

1. bed, bed, bear
   /bɛd/, /bɛd/, /bɛr/
2. tire, tired, tire
   /taʸr/, /taʸrd/, /taʸr/
3. what, where, where
   /wʌt/, /wɛr/, /wɛr/
4. explored, explore, explored
   /ɛksˈploʷrd/, /ɛksˈploʷr/, /ɛksˈploʷrd/
5. car, car, card
   /kɑr/, /kɑr/, /kɑrd/
6. share, share, shared
   /ʃɛr/, /ʃɛr/, /ʃɛrd/
7. are, art, are
   /ɑr/, /ɑrt/, /ɑr/
8. fear, feet, feet
   /fɪr/, /fɪʸt/, /fɪʸt/

Answer Key

	X	Y	Z
1.			✓
2.		✓	
3.	✓		
4.		✓	
5.			✓
6.			✓
7.		✓	
8.	✓		

🎧 D Saying final sounds /t/, /d/, and /r/
Class CD 2, Track 47

Now students practice saying the final /**t**/, /**d**/, and /**r**/ sounds they have been hearing. Have them listen to the words on the audio and repeat them at least two times.

> **Teaching tip** To help students say the difficult final cluster /**rd**/ ("card," "shared"), have them practice saying word pairs that have this consonant cluster where the words link. For example, ask students to repeat the following phrases several times.
>
> car door
> her doll
> their dog
> far down

E Pair work: Present and past

Go over the time expressions in the box with students. It can be useful to have them repeat the expressions in unison several times. These expressions were introduced in Unit 10. They are very useful, but often confused. Then go over the instructions and example. Remind students to choose sentences **a** or **b** at random and to vary their responses.

This task helps students see the important relationship between word-final sounds and grammatical meaning.

> **Teaching tip** As in the Teaching Tip for Unit 10, Task D, on page 36 of this Teacher's Resource and Assessment Book, have students think of other words to use in these sentences. A lively class can be creative with this task by using unlikely words. For example:
>
> 1. They share(d)   a pizza.
>   a coat.
>   a joke.
>
> 2. I care(d) about   you.
>   my work.
>   football.
>
> 3. They prepare(d)   a cake.
>   a lesson.
>   a plan.
>
> 4. They fear(ed)   cats.
>   cars.
>   mice.
>
> 5. We repair(ed)   clocks.
>   glasses.
>   broken hearts.
>
> 6. Snakes scare(d)   birds.
>   dogs.
>   me.
>
> 7. I adore(d)   chocolate cake.
>   apple pie.
>   you.

🎧 F Linking with /r/
Class CD 2, Track 48

Linking practice is a good way to work on a difficult sound like /**r**/, because it may be easier to say at the beginning or the end of a word, depending on the rules of students' first languages. Remind students to link their hands together while they are saying the linking sounds.

G Linking with /r/, /t/, /d/, and /l/
Class CD 2, Track 49

This task aims to integrate the linking skills students practiced in the previous task with the linking with /l/ they practiced in Unit 9 and the linking with /t/ and /d/ they practiced in Unit 8.

Because the /r/, /t/, /d/, and /l/ linking sounds may sound similar in students' first languages, remind them to listen carefully for the differences between these sounds. Then play the audio, and have students repeat the sentences at least two times.

H Pair work: What does "roar" mean?

Go over the instructions and examples with students. Then have them do the exercise in pairs. Remind them to select sentences **a** or **b** at random. Use the illustrations provided to help them understand new vocabulary.

Note: As mentioned on page 37 of this Teacher's Resource and Assessment Book, the /r/ sound has an effect on the previous vowel sound, so that "pair" /pɛr/ and "paid" /peʸd/ have rather different vowel qualities. On the other hand, the words "her" /hər/ and "hurt" /hərt/ have different vowel *letters* but nonetheless, have the same vowel sound. This tends to confuse students. Urge them to rely on their ears, not their eyes, and remind them to pay special attention to the final sound.

I Music of English
Class CD 2, Track 50

Working with "what" /wʌt/ and "where" /wɛr/ reinforces the work students have been doing on learning to distinguish final /t/, /d/, and /r/. "What" and "where" also have different vowel sounds, but it is more important for students to concentrate on the final consonant difference.

J Pair work: What is it? Where is it?

Have students first quickly read the two lists headed "What?" and "Where?" in the boxes on page 82 of the Student's Book. Practice any words you think may be new for students by pointing to the relevant picture and asking, "What is it?" or "Where is it?" Then go over the instructions and examples with students, and have them do the exercise in pairs.

K Music of English
Class CD 2, Track 51

Ask students if they ever have trouble remembering the word for something in their own language, and if so, what general words they use instead. Tell them that, in English, the general words "thing" and "stuff" are useful for people with limited vocabulary. However, explain that "stuff" is more colloquial and shouldn't be used in formal situations.

Low-level students may not be ready to understand the abstract distinction between "countable" and "non-countable" nouns (e.g., "two pencils," "many books," but "some milk," and "some cheese"). However, even without knowing about this difference, it is useful for them to practice questions using the words "thing" (countable) and "stuff" (non-countable).

It is quite usual to say "um" or "uh" while thinking of a word. This hesitation sound means "I am not finished speaking yet, just thinking." It extends the speaker's turn briefly and is, therefore, more useful than just a pause.

After students listen to the audio and repeat the sentences, have them repeat the exchange at least once more as a whole piece, to show how the meanings of the sentences are connected.

L Pair work: Asking for more information
Class CD 2, Track 52

Have students listen to the conversation on the audio before they practice with each other. Remind them to emphasize the words in bold.

Note: Some people say "refrigerator," but the shorter version, "fridge" /frɪdʒ/, is quite common.

M Review: Most important words and strong syllables

In this task, students look for and focus on the most important word and its strong syllable in a word group.

> ### Answer Key
>
> strong syllable (green level):   *way*
> most important word (orange level): *away*

Unit 11 Quiz is available on page 82.

12 Continuing and Stop Sounds + /s/ or /z/
Linking with /s/ and /z/

What's a bank for?
Where's the library? It's on Main Street.

Unit overview

The main focus of this unit is on *consonant clusters* with final **/s/** or **/z/** sounds. Students will practice listening for and using these sounds as a plural marker for nouns, and as a reduced form of "is" in "What's," "Where's," and "It's."

Consonant clusters are difficult for students whose first languages do not place consonants together. Also, in some languages, few consonants can occur in the final position. This is one possible reason why the grammatically important final **/s/** or **/z/** is often not heard well or used in learner's speech.

∩ A Review: Final sounds /t/, /d/, /s/, and /z/
Class CD 3, Track 2

The aim of this task is to refresh students' memories of the sounds **/t/** and **/d/** and **/s/** and **/z/**, which were introduced in Unit 8. Have them listen to the audio and repeat the words at least two times.

∩ B Do you hear a final /s/ or /z/ sound?
Class CD 3, Track 3

As students listen to the audio, have them check whether they hear a final **/s/** or **/z/** sound or not.

Audio Script	
1. bus	/bʌs/
2. but	/bʌt/
3. has	/hæz/
4. hat	/hæt/
5. shop	/ʃɑp/
6. shops	/ʃɑps/
7. banks	/bæŋks/
8. bank	/bæŋk/
9. road	/roʷd/
10. roads	/roʷdz/

Answer Key		
	Yes	No
1.	✓	
2.		✓
3.	✓	
4.		✓
5.		✓
6.	✓	
7.	✓	
8.		✓
9.		✓
10.	✓	

∩ C Stop sounds + /s/ or /z/
Class CD 3, Track 4

In this task, students listen for the **/s/** or **/z/** ending after **stop sounds**. Remind them that final **/s/** or **/z/** is the crucial sound for signaling that an item is plural. The exact sound may be **/s/** or **/z/**, but the important teaching point is that students must make some kind of "hissing sound" where the word is spelled with a final letter **-s-**.

Have students listen to the audio and circle the words they hear.

Note: The plural ending is always spelled with the letter **-s-**, but it may be pronounced either as **/s/** or **/z/**. The difference is caused by the quality of the preceding consonant. If that consonant is *voiceless*, then the final letter **-s-** is pronounced **/s/** (e.g., "caps" /kæps/). However, if that consonant is *voiced*, then the final letter is pronounced **/z/** (e.g., "cabs" /kæbz/).

It is not necessary to explain this to beginning students, as it might confuse them. At this stage, it is enough to make them aware that there may be variations in sound for the letter **-s-**.

🎧 D Continuing sounds + /s/ or /z/
Class CD 3, Track 5

Now students listen for the /s/ or /z/ ending after continuing sounds. Have students listen to the audio and circle the words they hear.

Note: Items 4, 8, and 9 have silent letter -e- endings.

E Pair work: Is it one or more than one?

To introduce this task, draw a star on the left side of the board, and write the word "star" above it. Ask "How many?" When a student answers "one," write "one" beneath the star. Then draw several stars on the right side of the board, and write "stars" above them. Ask "How many?" Students may tell you any number of stars; accept their answers, and write "more than one" beneath the group of stars. Remind students how important the /s/ or /z/ sound is in English, because it indicates more than one.

Then read the directions out loud, and model the task by taking the part of Student A and choosing someone in the class to take the part of Student B. Have students repeat after you the names of the places in the box before you put the students into pairs to complete the task. Use the illustrations on pages 87 and 89 of the Student's Book to help explain what some of these places are.

🎧 F Review: Linking with /s/ or /z/
Class CD 3, Track 6

Have students listen to the audio and repeat each sentence at least two times.

Remind students that it is important to practice linking because it will make their speech more understandable and improve their listening comprehension. Also remind them that it is necessary to be attentive about hearing and saying the final /s/ or /z/ sounds, since they carry so much information.

∩ G Music of English
Class CD 3, Track 7

In this task, students integrate three things they have studied:

1. consonant clusters with /s/ ("what's," "it's")
2. using intonation to highlight the most important word in a sentence
3. linking with /s/ ("What's a," "it's for")

Have students listen to the audio and repeat each sentence at least two times.

It will help students' listening comprehension if they become aware of the way native English speakers systematically contract auxiliaries such as "is" in normal speech. For that reason, it is useful to practice saying "what's." However, this should be restricted to meaning "What is . . ." rather than "What does . . ." because beginning students have a tendency to say "What means that?" Instead of "What does that mean?" Therefore, practice with the contraction of "does" should be put off until a later stage.

H Pair work: What's a bank for?

Have students repeat after you the words in the "Places" and "Answers" boxes. Remind them to pay attention to the strong syllables in the words and the most important words in the sentences. Then read the instructions, and model the task by taking the part of Student A and choosing someone in the class to take the part of Student B.

"What's it for?" is a useful question for language learners because it gives them an easy way to find out the meaning of unknown vocabulary.

Note: Students may be confused by the similarity between "park" (the noun) and "parking." This exercise can help them distinguish the meanings of the two words.

∩ I Music of English
Class CD 3, Track 8

Tell students that the rest of the tasks in this unit will give them practice in asking for directions, a useful skill in a strange town. Have them listen to the audio and repeat each sentence at least two times. Remind students to pronounce the linking between the /s/ or /z/ sounds and the sounds that follow them.

∩ J Pair work: Giving locations
Class CD 3, Track 9

Have students listen to the audio. Then discuss the meanings of the expressions "on the corner of," "across the street," and "one block south" before students practice the conversation with a partner. It would be a

good idea to review the words for the four directions ("north," "south," "east," and "west"), represented by "N," "S," "E," and "W," before moving on to the next task.

Step 3 gives students some practice in listening to and then saying locations they can use when giving directions and in preparation for the map game in Task K, on pages 91–93 of the Student's Book.

Review the Two Vowel Rule and One Vowel Rule in preparation for Task K, using "Jean" and "Jen" as examples. The map game presents a challenge based on these vowel rules.

> **Teaching tip** If your students are able to manage more complex directions, they should be encouraged to think of other ways to give directions. The last direction in the examples below introduces the concept of describing cross streets.
>
> Examples:
> It's six blocks to the south of _____.
> It's on the northwest corner of _____.
> It's on _____ near _____.
> It's on _____ at _____.

K Game: Map challenge

In this extra activity, go over the names of the streets on the map on page 92 of the Student's Book. Then read the instructions and model the task by taking the part of Student A and choosing someone in the class to take the part of Student B. Remind students not to look at each other's maps.

You might want to remind students about the number of syllables in "store" and "street," as speakers of some Latin languages might have the tendency to add a vowel before /s/ + another consonant at the beginning of a word.

You might also want to remind students that, when giving street names, it isn't always necessary to say the word "street" (e.g., "It's on the corner of Main and Jen.").

> **Teaching tip** Another approach is to paint or draw a reusable map on a large piece of cloth or plastic sheeting, and have students take turns giving each other directions to walk to locations. This makes an entertaining physical activity and reinforces the need for vowel clarity.

Unit 12 Quiz is available on page 83.

13 Numbers
Checking and Correcting Mistakes

Did you say "ninety"? No, "nineteen." What does Mr. True sell?

Unit overview

This very practical unit focuses on numbers. Students will practice the distinction between the often-confused **-teen** and **-ty** number endings, and will practice saying telephone numbers. They will also review all of the different combinations of linking sounds they have learned so far.

Numbers are a necessary part of a new language, needed for everyday use. However, they are sometimes hard to remember because we all learned to count in our native language at a very early age, so we tend to think numerically in that language.

Similar-sounding pairs of numbers, like "thirteen" and "thirty," are especially confusing for students, so this unit introduces a verification / correction technique to help students confirm which one was said. The same technique is then applied to phone numbers.

A Saying numbers and years
Class CD 3, Track 10

Have students listen to the audio and repeat the numbers and years they hear at least two times. Students can trace the pitch lines in the boxes with their index finger as they listen, to reinforce the difference in the intonation patterns used for numbers ending in **-ty** and **-teen**.

If you have a class of students for whom personal questions about age are not a problem, you can write these questions on the board and have them ask each other "How old are you?" and "What year were you born?"

B Music of English
Class CD 3, Track 11

Have students listen to the audio and repeat each sentence at least two times.

Note: After students listen to the audio and repeat the sentences, have them repeat the exchange at least once more as a whole unit, to show how the meanings and intonation patterns of the sentences are linked.

C Pair work: Correcting a mistake about a number

Ask students, "In what situations do you need to hear numbers correctly?" (Sample answers: "at the bank," "when making appointments and reservations," "when shopping," etc.) Then ask, "Why is it important to check that you heard the correct number?" (Sample answers: "you may lose money," "you may not be able to communicate with someone," "you may miss a train," etc.) Remind students not to be shy about checking numbers they are not sure about, as the consequences can be serious!

Go over the instructions and examples with students. Tell them to choose from the pairs of numbers at random to keep this task interesting. This task asks students to pretend that they misheard a number. If doing so makes them uneasy, explain that it is an opportunity to practice verifying information when they are not sure what was just said.

Note: It may be helpful to explain that boldface type in the example conversations highlights the words and syllables that receive special emphasis. In these conversations the numbers are emphasized because the speakers are asking and correcting in order to confirm which numbers were said.

D Listening for pauses in telephone numbers
Class CD 3, Track 12

Have students listen to the audio and practice saying the telephone numbers. It can be useful to explain to students that there are conventional ways for grouping telephone numbers (as well as other numbers, such as credit card account numbers), and that it is difficult for listeners to understand numbers if they are not grouped according to local conventions. Anybody who has tried to get a telephone number from an operator in a foreign country is likely to have experienced this difficulty.

Each of these telephone numbers begins with an area code. As students listen to the numbers in this task, encourage them to tap their pencils or feet at the pauses.

⌒ E Saying telephone numbers
Class CD 3, Track 13

Have students listen to the audio and repeat the telephone numbers they hear at least two times. Then have them dictate their own phone number, or a fictitious one that they choose, to their partners and check what their partners wrote.

Note: The number combination "555" is used in this book to ensure that none of the phone numbers are real, as this combination is never found in real phone numbers in the United States.

> **Teaching tip** If you have an out-of-date or extra telephone directory, use it to give students more practice in saying phone numbers. Simply tear out a page for each student, and have them dictate three or more numbers on that page to their partners. They should then check what their partners wrote.

⌒ F Stores at the Seaside Mall
Class CD 3, Track 14

This task introduces a context in which students will be able to practice saying numbers. Before students listen to the audio, have them read the directory. The locations given in the directory show where each store is located within the mall, including the level, A, B, or C. Then have students listen to the audio and say the name of each store at least two times.

Note: The vowel letter in "mall" /mɔl/ does not follow the One Vowel Rule, but instead sounds like the vowel in "fall," "ball," "call," "coffee" /ˈkɔ•fiʸ/, or "soft" /sɔft/. This vowel sound is not included in the system of 11 vowels on which this course is based – alphabet vowels, relative vowels, and *schwa* – which are the most common vowels. A beginner's most urgent need is to have simple rules they can use to decode most words. Other vowels can be studied later.

⌒ G Music of English
Class CD 3, Track 15

The exchange "Where is Big Guy?" / "It's at twenty-five B." illustrates the customary signaling of the final element of a list of items with a lengthened vowel and a rise-fall in the pitch. Students learned this pattern when they studied spelling in Unit 4. The same pattern is used for the last letter in an acronym (e.g., "UN," "TV," "BBC," etc.) and the last number or word in a list.

"Nine" and "five" are frequently confused or misheard by students who tend not to notice final consonants.

Note: After students listen to the audio and repeat the sentences, have them repeat the exchange at least once more as a whole piece, to show how the meanings and intonation patterns of the sentences are linked.

⌒ H Pair work: Calling for information
Class CD 3, Track 16

Have students listen to the audio and then say the conversation at least two times with a partner. Have partners switch roles the second time they practice the conversation.

> **Teaching tip** This activity and the next one can be made more enjoyable and challenging by having students sit back-to-back. Encourage them to hold imaginary telephone receivers to their ears so that it feels more like they are actually having a telephone conversation. When they cannot see each other's mouths, they have to rely entirely on their ears.

I Pair work: Where is it? What's the telephone number?

Go over the instructions. Then model the example with a student. Have students take turns being the customer and the clerk. Student A can ask for the first seven phone numbers and locations, and Student B for the other seven.

A much more difficult task could be for a student to read a telephone number out loud, asking the partner to name the store that goes with that number. This is not a realistic situation, but if the students have done the other tasks without difficulty, they might enjoy a more challenging exercise.

> **Teaching tip** Here is a challenging – but very noisy – way to do this pair-work task with smaller classes. After going over the task instructions, have all Student As line up facing the right wall, and all Student Bs facing the left wall. Tell them to do the task from these positions. Students will have to speak very loudly and clearly and will have to concentrate hard on distinguishing their partners' voice. After students finish the task, let them meet with their partners to check their answers, but tell them they must check orally, without looking at each other's books.

J About the stores at the Seaside Mall
Class CD 3, Track 17

Ask students if they ever go to malls, and if so, what kinds of stores they see there. Then have students cover the right column of the Seaside Mall chart with a sheet of paper. Ask them to guess what each store sells. Some will be easy to guess (for example, "FastBurger" and "Speed Electronics"), but others, such as "Small World" and "The Old Oak," may inspire some creative guessing.

Tell students you are going to play the audio or read the script, and that they can uncover each answer in the chart *after* they hear it. Tell them that this information will prepare them to do the next two tasks.

Note: No store would advertise itself as "cheap" or "inexpensive" (which can imply low-quality goods), but instead it might use a term like "discount" or "factory outlet," which implies low prices.

K Music of English
Class CD 3, Track 18

This task not only practices question and answer intonation, but also reviews the distinction between the vowel sounds in "men" and "teen."

> **Teaching tip**   Try putting students in groups of four for further practice. Have two of the students say line 1 of the exchange *in unison*. This is challenging, because they have to speak together. Then have the other two students say line 2 in unison, and so on. Then they should switch roles. Speaking along with someone else can help shy students pronounce the lines more assertively.

L Pair work: Checking information
Class CD 3, Track 19

Have students listen to the conversation on the audio or as you read out loud and then practice the conversation at least two times with a partner. They should switch roles the second time they practice.

Then have them take turns being the customer and asking about what some of the stores at the Seaside Mall sell. The customers can get the names of the stores in Task F, on page 97 of the Student's Book. The clerk can find the answers in Task J, on page 100 of the Student's Book.

More advanced students might enjoy adding information about these stores (or inventing new stores) to quiz each other about.

Note: Although the standard pattern for "inexpensive" is to stress the third syllable, the clerk's emphasis is on the **first** syllable, because that contrast is the main point of her answer.

M More linking
Class CD 3, Track 20

Start by pointing out that this task gives examples of five different categories of linking. Go over each category, eliciting examples. Then have students listen to the audio and repeat each sentence at least two times. Point out the many different categories of linking that the students have learned.

Note: Linking with the word "is" often results in a contraction, dropping the vowel altogether. For example:

Smart Woman's inexpensive.
Gemstone's expensive.

N Review: Correcting mistakes

In this task, students are asked to think about which word is the most important and which syllable of that word is the most important. They are also being reminded of the importance of the vowel in that syllable.

You might want to notice that the sentence in item 2 answers the question in item 1 and that the sentence in item 4 answers the question in item 3, thus the stress on the first syllable of "inexpensive" for emphasis.

Answer Key	
1. strong syllable:	nine
most important word:	ninety
2. strong syllable:	teen
most important word:	nineteen
3. strong syllable:	pen
most important word:	expensive
4. strong syllable:	in
most important word:	inexpensive

Unit 13 Quiz is available on page 84.

14 Final Sounds /n/, /l/, /nd/, and /ld/
Linking with /n/, /l/, /nd/, and /ld/

What's a trail?
It's a path.

Unit overview

In this unit, students will practice distinguishing between and pronouncing the final sounds /**n**/, /**l**/, /**nd**/, and /**ld**/. When the final consonant cluster ends with a /**d**/, it sometimes means "past tense," so it is important to hear it accurately. Students will also work on linking with these sounds and practice checking and correcting information.

A Final sounds /n/, /l/, and /d/

For students from some language backgrounds, it is difficult to learn to make the difference between /**n**/, /**l**/, and /**d**/. Even if a student has no difficulty distinguishing /**n**/ from /**l**/, many languages do not allow consonant clusters. Since English uses a lot of consonant clusters, most students need practice with final consonant combinations. Since final /**l**/ + /**d**/ often serve as grammar cues, the tasks which combine these sounds with other consonants are particularly important.

Before teaching this unit, take some time to use a mirror (and perhaps a flashlight) to look into your own mouth. You will see the soft part of the roof of your mouth hanging down at the back. This is the ***velum,*** or ***soft palate.***

Most of the time, the velum hangs down so that air can flow down through the nose into the lungs for breathing. But when you are speaking, the velum closes off the airflow from the nose so that air flows out of the mouth.

For nasal sounds like /**n**/ and /**ŋ**/, however, the airflow out of the mouth is stopped, and the velum drops down to allow the air to flow out of the nose instead.

Therefore the most important difference between the /**n**/ and the non-nasal /**l**/ and /**d**/ sounds is that, for /**n**/, the velum is down. The most important difference between /**l**/ and /**d**/ is that /**l**/ is a ***continuing sound*** and /**d**/ is a ***stop***, as covered in Unit 9. A practical approach to teaching students to pronounce these three sounds

correctly is to give the class a lot of practice listening to the three different sounds and looking at the pictures of the different tongue positions and airflow patterns. You may want to follow these steps:

1. Ask students to look at the pictures comparing /**n**/ and /**d**/. Point out that the tongue is actually in the same position, but the difference is in the way the air flows out. No air flows out of the mouth for either sound but, for /**n**/, it does flow out of the nose. Let students experiment with the words "in," "fine," and "cone" so that they feel the free flow of air through their noses (unless they have colds, in which case the words may sound like "id," "fide," and "code").

2. Next, have students try out contrasting /**n**/ and /**d**/ with pairs of words, such as "Ben" / "bed," "ten" / "Ted," until they can feel the difference between a total stoppage of air versus air flowing through the nose.

3. When students understand the difference between /**n**/ and /**d**/, use the pictures to show how the airflow is different for the /**l**/ and /**n**/ sounds. For the /**l**/ sound, the air flows out of the mouth; for the /**n**/ sound, the air flows out of the nose. The mirror test in Task K on page 108 of the Student's Book can also help. (Try this out yourself before you present it to the students.) But /**l**/ and /**n**/ are also distinguished by their different tongue positions, as students can see in the pictures. Point this out to your students.

🎧 B Listening for final sounds /n/ and /l/
Class CD 3, Track 21

Have students listen to the audio and circle the words they hear. Some of these words are defined in Task H. However, at this point in the course, students don't need to know the meanings of these words. The purpose of the task is just to train their ears to hear the final sound distinction.

C Which word do you hear?
Class CD 3, Track 22

Audio Script

1. bone   /bo^wn/
2. rain   /re^yn/
3. mail   /me^yl/
4. well   /wɛl/
5. fine   /fɑ^yn/
6. pain   /pe^yn/
7. trail   /tre^yl/
8. tell   /tɛl/

Answer Key

1. (bone)   bowl
2. (rain)   rail
3. main   (mail)
4. when   (well)
5. (fine)   file
6. (pain)   pail
7. train   (trail)
8. ten   (tell)

D Which word is different?
Class CD 3, Track 23

Audio Script

1. ten, tell, ten
   /tɛn/, /tɛl/, /tɛn/
2. rain, rail, rail
   /re^yn/, /re^yl/, /re^yl/
3. when, well, when
   /wɛn/, /wɛl/, /wɛn/
4. pin, pin, pill
   /pɪn/, /pɪn/, /pɪl/
5. win, will, win
   /wɪn/, /wɪl/, /wɪn/
6. coal, cone, coal
   /ko^wl/, /ko^wn/, /ko^wl/
7. fine, fine, file
   /fɑ^yn/, /fɑ^yn/, /fɑ^yl/
8. bowl, bone, bowl
   /bo^wl/, /bo^wn/, /bo^wl/

Answer Key

	X	Y	Z
1.		✓	
2.	✓		
3.		✓	
4.			✓
5.		✓	
6.		✓	
7.			✓
8.		✓	

E Saying final sounds /n/ and /l/
Class CD 3, Track 24

Have students listen to the audio and repeat each word at least two times.

Note: Just as with /r/, the sound /l/ can affect the sound of a preceding vowel sound. That is why the vowels in pairs such as "can" /kæn/ and "call" /kɔl/ do not sound exactly the same.

F Saying final sounds /nd/ and /ld/
Class CD 3, Track 25

Have students listen to the audio and repeat each word at least two times.

Note: Encourage students to use their ears, not their eyes, to judge the number of syllables in words such as "filed" or "phoned."

G Music of English
Class CD 3, Track 26

After students listen to the audio and repeat the sentences, have them repeat the exchange at least once more as a whole piece, to show how the meanings and intonation patterns of the sentences are linked.

Also remind them that the words "thing" (countable noun) and "stuff" (non-countable noun) are especially useful for people with limited vocabulary. See Unit 11, Task K, on page 39 of this Teacher's Resource and Assessment Book for information on the distinction between "thing" and "stuff."

H Pair work: What's a train for?

Go over the instructions, modeling the examples with a student. Then put students into pairs, and have them do the pair work. Remind them to choose questions **a** or **b** at random to keep the task challenging.

Note: Less familiar words, such as "fold," are included to encourage students to practice asking the meaning or spelling of a new word and also to notice the final consonant or consonant cluster (e.g., /ld/). In this case, you can also point out that because "fold" ends in /d/, it will gain an extra syllable for the -ed ending in the past tense. On the other hand, the verb "phone" does not end in either /d/ or /t/, so it does not have an extra syllable for the -ed ending in the past tense. The rules concerning the past tense -ed ending are presented in Unit 5, on page 35 of the Student's Book.

> **Teaching tip**   This task gives students the opportunity to practice pronouncing these final sounds in sentences. For further practice in pronouncing final /n/ *linked* to a following word, students can suggest a list of objects for you to write on the board (e.g., "computer," "car," "bicycle," etc.). Then ask three or four other students, "Do you own a ____?" At the end, tally the number of persons owning these objects.

I Linking with /l/, /n/, /ld/, and /nd/
Class CD 3, Track 27

Have students listen to the audio and repeat the words and sentences at least two times.

You could ask students to find the four instances of final silent letter -e- before they listen: "phone," "called," "are," "spelled."

Note: The sound /l/ in "call" is a continuing sound, so the linking can be made by drawing out the sound in an exaggerated link. But /d/ is a stop sound, so "Hold on" and "Spend it" run together abruptly, causing the last words to sound like "don" and "dit."

J Pair work: Checking information
Class CD 3, Track 28

Have students listen to the audio and then say the conversations at least two times. The second time they say the conversations, they should switch roles.

These dialogues are meant to reinforce the use of intonational emphasis to confirm information or correct misunderstandings. This is the way native English speakers help the listener follow. Without this crucial signal, the listener might miss the speaker's meaning, causing a breakdown in communication.

> **Teaching tip**   These dialogues could be acted out as brief skits, if the students are advanced enough, requiring students to memorize the lines and then concentrate on how to say them.

K The mirror test: Final sounds /n/ and /l/

This task is meant to help students who are having difficulty producing word-final /n/ and /l/ correctly.

To do this activity, you will need to have several small mirrors. A compact cosmetic mirror will work fine, and some students may actually have these with them.

A cold mirror works best to condense the moisture from the airflow, so this test may not work well on a hot day. Also, it is easier to see the "cloud" distinction when using individual sounds than to see it when using words. A word that ends in /l/ may cause some slight clouding of the mirror, but a word that ends in /n/ will cause much more clouding.

Students may find the following anatomical fact interesting: Some noses make two clouds, but some make just one cloud.

To help students see the clouding more clearly, you could ask them to say the /n/ with force, "like a dragon breathing fire."

Another way to use the mirror is to ask students to hold it in front of their mouths and to watch themselves as they say the sounds. When they say /l/, they should be able to see a space on either side of the tip of the tongue for air to come out. When they say /n/, they should not be able to see any space for air to come out (it can only come out of the nose) because the tongue closes the mouth exit in the same way as for the stop sounds /d/ or /t/.

Yet another way to sense the difference between the two sounds is to gently hold the bridge of the nose (near the base of the bony part) with thumb and forefinger, without squeezing. The nose should vibrate when they say /n/ and not vibrate when they say /l/.

Try these techniques yourself before presenting them to the class.

Unit 14 Quiz is available on page 85.

15 Final Sounds /s/, /θ/, and /t/
Linking with /θ/

What's a bath for?
To get clean.

Unit overview

The sound **/θ/** is spelled with the letters **-th-** and is typically difficult for many students, so substitution of other sounds is common.

In this unit, students will practice distinguishing between and pronouncing the final sounds **/s/**, **/θ/**, and **/t/**. They will also practice linking with **/θ/**, continue to practice the skills of checking and correcting information, and review all the categories of linking they have learned in this course.

A Final sounds /s/, /θ/, and /t/
Class CD 3, Track 29

When attempting to say the English **/θ/** sound, which is a relatively rare sound in the world's languages, some students tend to substitute **/t/** (e.g., "tank you"), and others substitute **/s/** (e.g., "sank you"), depending on the phonology of their first language.

1. Call students' attention to the mouth illustrations. In the "Looking to the front" pictures, point out the area that shows the shape of the mouth opening. Students can see clearly how different the flat tongue shape is for **/θ/**, in contrast to the v-shaped channel for **/s/** and the complete blockage for **/t/**.

   Give them lots of time to experiment with making these sounds while looking at the pictures. The better they can understand what their mouths should be doing, the more clearly they will be able to make the sounds. Then play the audio.

2. Point out to students the difference of the vowel sound in "boss" /bɔs/ vs. the vowel sound in "both" /boʷθ/ and "boat" /boʷt/.

Note: /θ/ is not really a crucial sound for beginners, because it is not used to convey a grammatical signal. However, it is included here because the voiced version is so common in English (e.g., "the," "them," etc.), and so many students worry about it. These mouth images make clear how differently this sound is made from how the other common substitutes, **/t/** and **/s/**, are made. The higher-level book in this series, *Clear Speech*, deals with voicing and thus teaches both the /θ/ and /ð/ sounds.

B Which word do you hear?
Class CD 3, Track 30

Have students listen to the audio and circle the words they hear. Alternatively, to give students a chance to work in a more active mode, have them respond to each word by holding up a hand for "stop" or drawing a line in the air for "continue."

Audio Script

1.	both	/boʷθ/
2.	path	/pæθ/
3.	mat	/mæt/
4.	Beth	/bɛθ/
5.	fort	/foʷrt/
6.	night	/nɑʸt/
7.	rice	/rɑʸs/
8.	fate	/feʸt/
9.	with	/wɪθ/
10.	race	/reʸs/

Answer Key

1.	(both)	boat
2.	(path)	pat
3.	mass	(mat)
4.	(Beth)	bet
5.	force	(fort)
6.	nice	(night)
7.	(rice)	right
8.	face	(fate)
9.	(with)	wit
10.	(race)	rate

C Which word is different?

In this task, students practice listening for the difference between final /s/, /θ/, and /t/. The final sounds /s/ and /θ/ can be difficult to distinguish, especially on audio, even for native English speakers.

Audio Script

1. boat, both, boat
   /boʷt/, /boʷθ/, /boʷt/
2. bath, bath, bat
   /bæθ/, /bæθ/, /bæt/
3. mass, mass, math
   /mæs/, /mæs/, /mæθ/
4. nice, night, night
   /naʸs/, /naʸt/, /naʸt/
5. rate, rate, race
   /reʸt/, /reʸt/, /reʸs/
6. rice, rice, right
   /raʸs/, /raʸs/, /raʸt/
7. mouth, mouth, mouse
   /maʷθ/, /maʷθ/, /maʷs/
8. fourth, fort, fourth
   /foʷrθ/, /foʷrt/, /foʷrθ/

Answer Key

	X	Y	Z
1.		✓	
2.			✓
3.			✓
4.	✓		
5.			✓
6.			✓
7.			✓
8.		✓	

D Saying final /θ/ (-th-)

As students look again at the illustration of a mouth saying /θ/, point out how flat the tongue is as the air flows over it. Then play the audio, and have students repeat each word at least two times.

This is the first time that students are being asked to say the /θ/ sound out loud, and some of them may feel awkward or self-conscious about it. You can help them relax by being a bit silly yourself. Model the pronunciation of these words, but exaggerate the final /θ/; make it extra loud and long.

Note: It is better not to ask students to stick their tongues out between their teeth. This is disturbing for many people and is not necessary to make the sound clearly.

Teaching tip Here is another way to help students distinguish between the pronunciation of the /s/ and /θ/ sounds. Have them say the sounds and hold each one for several seconds. As they say the sounds, they should hold their hands or a piece of tissue about an inch away from their mouths. When they say /θ/, they will feel their breath on their fingers, or the tissue will flutter. When they say /s/, they will feel almost no breath on their fingers, or the tissue will stay nearly still.

E Saying final sounds /θ/, /t/, and /d/ in numbers

Play the audio and have students repeat each number at least two times.

Teaching tip Go around the room and have each student state his or her birthday using ordinal numbers (e.g., "first," "second," "third"). The other students should write down the birthdays they hear. Make a note of the birthdays as students say them, and when they are all finished, write the birthdays on the board so students can check what they wrote.

F Saying final sounds /s/, /z/, /θ/, and /t/

Have students listen to the audio and repeat each word at least two times.

Teaching tip Another way to practice the final sounds /s/, /z/, /θ/, and /t/ is to focus on the vowel sounds in words that end with them. When students' attention is diverted to another element, it makes the practice more difficult and more like the demands of an actual conversation in which the subject matter distracts from attention to pronunciation.

Review the Two Vowel Rule and One Vowel Rule on pages 19 and 20 of the Student's Book. Write words with final /s/ or /z/ on the board, and set up two columns of answer blanks beneath them, one for *alphabet vowel sounds* and one for *relative vowel sounds*.

Alphabet Vowels	Relative Vowels
/eʸ/ _____	/æ/ _____
/iʸ/ _____	/ɛ/ _____
/aʸ/ _____	/ɪ/ _____
/oʷ/ _____	/ɑ/ _____
/uʷ/ _____	/ʌ/ _____

Words with final /s/ or /z/:

base	/s/	please	/z/	has	/z/
rice	/s/	is	/z/	dress	/s/
nose	/z/	us	/s/	fuse	/z/

Ask students to look at the words and write them in the correct columns. Then ask students to say the words. Repeat the procedure with final /θ/ and /t/.

Words with final /θ/:

bath	faith	teeth	with
both	Seth	truth	math

Words with final /t/:

cute	bat	bait	it	boat
but	not	beat	bet	write

Note: There are no common words for some combinations of vowel sounds + final sounds.

∩ G Music of English
Class CD 3, Track 35

A "bat" is also used for cricket. Use whichever game is better known by your students.

H Pair work: What's a bath for?

This task is a review of a few useful sentences students have learned so far in this course. Since the word order of the auxiliary "do" is particularly difficult for students to master, repeated practice of this sort of construction is important.

Note: The word "bass," meaning a fish, is pronounced /bæs/, whereas the musical instrument "bass" is pronounced /be^{y}s/ for historical reasons. Here, the first pronunciation is used to pair with "bath."

> **Teaching tip** Play Bingo to help students practice the distinction between /s/, /θ/, and /t/. Here's how:
>
> 1. Make Bingo cards with grids of four columns across and four rows down on each card. Each card should have 16 empty boxes or cells. Fill the boxes with words from the list below. Use a different selection of words, or put them in a different order on each card. Give each student a small pile of beans or something else they can use as markers.
>
> | bass | mass | boss | bath |
> |------|------|------|------|
> | math | both | bat | mat |
> | boat | fours | fourth | fort |
> | rice | path | face | right |
> | pat | fate | race | mouse |
> | faith | rat | mouth | pass |

2. Direct students to mark the word they hear.
3. Have a student (the caller) call out the words from the list in random order (or read them out loud yourself).
4. The first student to get four words in a row (across or down) should call out "Bingo!" loud enough for everyone to hear.
5. Check with the class to see if that student is correct, that is, if all four words have actually been called out. If they have, that student is the next caller, calling out words in random order.

I Pair work: Checking days and dates

First, it might be helpful to say the lists of days and months, having students repeat after you, as some of these words may be new to some of them. After this, go over the instructions, modeling the examples with a student. Then put students into pairs and have them do the pair work. Remind them to choose from the different columns at random to keep the task interesting.

Note: When /θ/ is the final sound in the answers with dates, it should be said clearly. This is particularly important when verifying or confirming information. Also, if this word is the focus of information (*the most important word*), then the clarity of all parts of the word is extremely important.

> **Teaching tip** Make two different versions of a calendar for the next month (or ask students to make them), entering different school events, birthdays, or holidays on each one.
>
> Put students into pairs. Student A gets a copy of one calendar, and Student B gets the other. They should then ask each other for information, as they did in the map exercise in Unit 12, Task K, on pages 91–93 of the Student's Book.
>
> For a more challenging activity, distribute copies of a calendar of events (from a website or newspaper), and have students fill in separate (blank) calendars with three or four events to ask or tell each other about.

∩ J Linking with /θ/
Class CD 3, Track 36

Have students listen to the audio and repeat the phrases and sentences they hear until they can say them easily.

No examples are given of linking /θ/ to a following /s/ sound because it would tend to be frustrating at this level (e.g., "bath" + "soap").

K Review: Linking
Class CD 3, Track 37

This task reviews linking for many different sound combinations and linking when there is more than one link in a sentence.

Have students listen to the audio and repeat each sentence at least two times. Note that when the same sound is at the end of one word and the beginning of the next (e.g., "stop pushing"), the sound is not said two times, but simply takes longer to say.

Teaching tip   The sentences in this linking task can also be used to review syllable number. Ask students to count the numbers of syllables in each sentence. They should then compare their answers with a partner. Since missing (or added) syllables is such a common error, it is helpful to focus attention on this subject whenever there is time left in a lesson.

Organize students into small teams. Give each team a short paragraph from a website, magazine, or newspaper, and tell them to look for five good spots for linking words. Have them practice these links and then perform them for another team.

Each team should then experiment with the other teams' set of links.

Unit 15 Quiz is available on page 86.

52   Unit 15 *Final Sounds /s/, /θ/, and /t/ • Linking with /θ/*

16 Review

Unit overview

This unit gives students a chance to review and consolidate everything they have learned in this course. It also includes a series of "Check yourself" tasks so students can find out how much they have accomplished and what areas they still need to work on. The dialogues and Music of English tasks are a bit more extended than those in earlier units, so students should be able to sense how much they have progressed. If you have used the Clear Listening Diagnostic Test at the beginning of the course and have taught all the elements tested on it, you can now use the test again to check and show progress.

A Counting syllables: The Sunshine Café
Class CD 3, Track 38

Have students look at the menu for the Sunshine Café. Tell them to read the menu while they listen to the audio and then to answer the questions in step 2. This menu will be used for subsequent tasks that will serve to review all the various elements of spoken language that have been taught in this course.

The following is the syllabification for the words in the menu:

The San Fran•cis•co
fish, a•vo•ca•do, lett•uce, to•ma•toes, and art•i•choke

The Hon•o•lu•lu
roas•ted chick•en, pine•app•le, red on•ions, and may•o•nnaise

The To•ron•to
smoked chick•en, roas•ted bell pepp•ers, and cream cheese

The Dall•as
bar•be•cued beef, hot pepp•ers, and on•ions

The New York
corned beef, pick•les, to•ma•toes, and mus•tard

The L•A
cheese, sun•dried to•ma•toes, cu•cum•bers, and butt•er

Plain sand•wich•es
pea•nut butt•er and jell•y
tu•na sal•ad
egg sal•ad

Choice of fresh•ly baked bread
white, whole wheat, rye, French roll

Bev•erag•es (silent -e- in the second syllable)
co•ffee, tea, iced tea, milk, lem•o•nade, juice, spark•ling wa•ter

---

Teaching tip   To start a discussion about what students like in sandwiches, ask them to count which of these ingredients (foods) they have actually eaten. They may have eaten some of these ingredients without knowing what they were called. If students are not sure what some of these foods are, ask other students to explain, but if they cannot, there are some "definitions" below to help them. Using these food names in discussions ("What do you like in your sandwiches?") can help them learn the vocabulary and pronunciation before they fill in the chart on page 118 of the Student's Book.

Sandwich Ingredients:

1. "Hot peppers" do not have a high temperature, but they have a spicy flavor. "Bell peppers" are somewhat sweet, not spicy.
2. "Barbecued beef" is cooked with a sauce, usually made of tomatoes and brown sugar. "Corned beef" is preserved with salt and spices.
3. "Roasted chicken" is baked in an oven. "Smoked chicken" is cooked slowly over a wood fire. (Students may be more familiar with "fried chicken," which is fried in deep fat. It is common in fast-food restaurants, but not usually an ingredient of sandwiches.)
4. "Pickles" are cucumbers that have been placed in salt water or vinegar for a long time. "Mayonnaise" is a white, creamy sauce used on sandwich bread or in salads.

B Sounds and syllables chart

This task gives students a sense of how much they have learned during the course. The chart tests their grasp of some of the basic concepts covered in Units 1–15: alphabet vowels and relative vowels, syllable number and strength, and the distinction between stops and continuing sounds.

Have students write at least two words from the menu in each box in the chart. Tell them that there are many possible answers for each box, and that they can use the same word more than once. They can work individually, in pairs, or in groups. As they are working, copy the chart (without the examples and instructions) onto the board. Either have students go to the board and fill in the boxes, or elicit answers from the whole class when they are finished.

Answer Key

	One syllable		Two syllables		Three syllables
Two Vowel Rule Underline the alphabet vowel.	baked smoked beef plain whole iced tea	these cream cheese white wheat juice	roasted peanut		artichoke pineapple mayonnaise barbecued lemonade
One Vowel Rule Underline the relative vowel.	fish bell egg milk	red hot French	peppers chicken mustard jelly coffee	lettuce pickles butter salad	lemonade sandwiches artichoke pineapple cucumbers
Strong syllables Underline the strong syllable.	white		peppers chicken mustard sparkling salad jelly sun-dried peanut	lettuce pickles butter roasted coffee onions water	sandwiches artichoke tomatoes barbecued pineapple cucumbers mayonnaise
Final stop sounds Underline the final stop sound.	hot baked smoked iced egg white	milk red bread corned wheat	mustard roasted sun-dried peanut salad		artichoke barbecued lemonade
Final continuing sounds Underline the final continuing sound.	bell juice cheese plain tea whole	fish cream beef choice roll mile	chicken onions pickles jelly coffee sparkling	lettuce peppers butter tuna water	mayonnaise sandwiches tomatoes pineapple cucumbers

C Music of English
Class CD 3, Track 39

On the audio, students will hear the conversation as a whole piece, rather than broken up into lines. Have them listen and then practice the whole conversation with a partner at least two times. They should switch roles the second time they practice.

D Pair work: The most important word
Class CD 3, Track 40

Play the audio for the students, then have them underline what they think is the most important word in each word group.

Some answers may vary. Tell students that this is not a problem, as people's ideas of what word is most important can differ. However, you might point out that **structure words** (like "the," "and," "to") are not usually the most important words, unless there is some special meaning. You might also want to point out that if a single word like "Yes," "No," "OK" is followed by a comma or period, it is a full thought group, with its own focus of meaning.

Answer Key

1. Customer: I'd like the <u>Toronto</u>, please.
   Server: The <u>Toronto</u>?
   Customer: <u>Yes</u>, on whole <u>wheat</u>.
   Server: <u>OK</u>. One <u>Toronto</u>, on whole <u>wheat</u>. Coming <u>right</u> up!

2. Customer: I'd like the <u>Honolulu</u>, please.
   Server: <u>OK</u>, one <u>Honolulu</u>. What kind of <u>bread</u>?
   Customer: Whole <u>wheat</u>. <u>No</u>, I changed my <u>mind</u>. I'd like the <u>San Francisco</u>.
   Server: One San <u>Francisco</u>. On a French <u>roll</u>?
   Customer: That sounds <u>good</u>.
   Server: And to <u>drink</u>?
   Customer: <u>Tea</u>.
   Server: <u>Hot</u> tea?
   Customer: <u>No</u>, <u>iced</u> tea.
   Server: <u>Thank</u> you.

E Pair work: Finding the most important word

Have students read the conversations, and then, with a partner, underline the words they think are most important. Remind them that it is not a problem if their answers are slightly different, but that, when one speaker is correcting something the other speaker said, the corrected word is always stressed.

Teaching tip An excellent way for students to check their ability to make clear which words are important is to have Student A underline the most important words in a dialogue and then read it out loud to Student B, without showing Student B which words were marked. Student B should then mark the words he or she thinks were emphasized, and show the results to Student A. This kind of checking works best with a short dialogue (or paragraph) that the partners have not previously practiced. The listener's focus should be not on what words he or she would emphasize, but to listen for the word the speaker actually *did* emphasize. If the listener is uncertain, a question mark can be placed next to the sentence.

It can work very well to have one student read out loud to the whole class, and have them all mark the emphasis they think they heard. Because emphasis ("topic focus") is signaled in different ways by different languages, students need as much practice as possible doing it according to the specific English system.

Answer Key

1. The Happy Customer
Customer: What's the <u>best</u> sandwich?
Server: The <u>Honolulu</u>.
Customer: Is that the one with <u>pineapple</u>?
Server: <u>Yes</u>. And <u>chicken</u>.
Customer: <u>Smoked</u> chicken?
Server: <u>No</u>, <u>roasted</u> chicken.
Customer: That sounds <u>fine</u>!

2. A Problem with Lunch
Customer: I'd like the San <u>Francisco</u>, please.
Server: No <u>fish</u> today.
Customer: <u>Well</u>, then I'd like the <u>Toronto</u>.
Server: No <u>chicken</u> today.
Customer: Do you have <u>anything</u>?
Server: <u>Cheese</u>. But the cheese is <u>bad</u>.
Customer: Then just bring me <u>coffee</u>.

F Music of English
Class CD 3, Track 41

Again, students will hear the conversation as a whole piece, rather than broken up into sentences. After they listen, have them repeat the conversation at least two times. They should switch roles the second time they practice.

Have students practice this conversation with several partners. Because everybody – even speakers with the same first language – has a somewhat different way of speaking, it is important for students to learn to tolerate variations in what they hear. If learners hear exactly the same model each time (in a recording, for instance), they will not be so able to adjust to the actual conditions of real conversation in the new language.

> **Teaching tip** After the students have practiced the conversation in the Music of English box, ask them to substitute some of the words with items from the menu on page 117 of the Student's Book.
>
> If you have access to some authentic English-language menus and you feel that your class is ready for the challenge, make enough copies of the menus for each pair of students.
>
> Encourage students to be dramatic or humorous when doing this pair work. For example, they may want to make the customer very demanding, asking for things that are not on the menu, or they may want to make the server very stubborn. If time allows, let students write their conversations as skits, practice them, and perform them for the whole class. This could be an enjoyable final class activity.

G Working with the pyramid

Students have experienced simplified pyramid tasks, using a sample pyramid as a model. Now they are being asked to fill out pyramids for two different sentences, without a model.

> **Answer Key**
>
> 1. strong syllable   Dal
>   most important word   Dallas
> 2. strong syllable   ron
>   most important word   Toronto

H Check yourself: Syllables, linking, and most important words

For the three tasks (Tasks H, I, and J, on pages 122–127 of the Student's Book), the procedure is the same.

It is best if each pair of students can record the dialogue. Then they should listen to the recording three times, each time completing a different checklist. You could assign

this as out-of-class work, if it proves impossible to have the proper recording equipment in class for all pairs of students. In addition, it is best for students to record their conversations in places without much background noise.

If recording equipment is available, students can work in groups of three. Two students will say the conversation at least three times while a third student listens and completes the checklists. If you use this method, be sure that listening students have the chance to do the speaking part of the task as well.

I Check yourself: Final sounds, linking, and most important words

Follow the procedure in Task H above.

J Review: Syllables, linking, and most important words

Follow the procedure in Task H above.

> **Teaching tip** If possible, record a short segment from a television drama (or download a free video clip from the Internet), and prepare a script of the segment for students to read. A soap opera is best because it usually has slow-paced, but natural, language and is likely to be dramatic. Then follow these steps:
>
> 1. Play the segment several times without sound, and ask students to notice the "body language." They should focus on emphasis, which may just be shown in the face, but may also involve more of the body in dramatic scenes.
> 2. Play the segment with the sound on.
> 3. Play it again, and have students read the script and circle the most important words.
> 4. Have students practice each line in a choral fashion, perhaps walking around the room and emphasizing the most important words with a long, swooping step on the strong syllable.
> 5. If students can say the sentences with confidence, put them into small groups to practice playing the scene.
> 6. Now they can perform the scene for the class.

Final Advice

As your students finish the course and you say good-bye, leave them with a parting message such as:

"If you are speaking with someone and they do not understand you, stop for a moment and think about the sentence you just said. You will not have time to try to say each sound again correctly, since the other person may be in a hurry, so the best way to help him or her understand is to decide which word was most important. Then say the sentence again, and make sure that you have made the strong syllable in that word very strong. Make the vowel in that syllable longer. And be sure that you make your voice go up or down. This is the best way to make sure you are speaking English clearly.

And if you are not sure what somebody said to you, ask them to repeat it. Listen for the most important word. If it is not clear, ask them about that word. Ask the questions you practiced in the Music of English tasks. Ask them, 'Did you say _____?' or 'What does _____ mean?' Your English is going to get better and better!"

Appendix A
Parts of the Mouth

This illustration shows an interior side view of the mouth. Students are generally not consciously aware of what is happening inside their mouths, so looking at illustrations of different perspectives can help. The following procedure can help students orient themselves to the "geography" of the inside of their mouths. Before doing it, familiarize yourself with the drawing in Appendix A on page 129 of the Student's Book. Give students time at each step to become consciously aware of the different parts of the *vocal tract*.

1 **Nose** – Draw just a nose on the board, facing to the right, the same way as in the illustration. Say "nose" as you draw it.

2 **Upper lip** – Continue the line down from the nose to draw an upper lip, saying, "upper lip." Ask students to touch the tip of their tongues to their upper lips. (There is no need for them to actually stick their tongues out beyond their upper lips.) Because this is a silent and private activity, even shy students should feel comfortable taking part. However, do not insist that students do this; they may simply wish to observe. After this, have students repeat after you the names of the parts so far: nose, upper lip, tongue, tip.

3 **Front teeth** – Continue the line, and draw the front teeth (rather v-shaped when looked at from the side). Say "front teeth," and ask students to follow with the tips of their tongues down the front of the teeth and up the back of the teeth.

4 **Tooth ridge** – Now extend the line slightly up and back from the teeth to show the tooth ridge (*alveolar ridge*). Say "tooth ridge," and ask them to follow this shape with their tongues, up over the bump behind the teeth and up to the roof of the mouth. Many English sounds are made by touching the tongue to the tooth ridge, for example, (/n/, /l/, /t/, or /d/). Other sounds are made by bringing the tongue near the tooth ridge, for example /s/ or /z/.

Appendix B
Vowel Rules

The vowel rules are reviewed here, and then lists of words are given so that students can have the opportunity to practice "sounding out" unfamiliar words. Students may recognize words they have heard but have never read. After students have learned about *strong syllables* in Unit 5, you can point out that the vowel rules work best in strong syllables.

A Review of vowel rules

Remind students of the Two Vowel Rule and the One Vowel Rule. Then you can say the words in the boxes out loud, and the students can repeat them.

B More words that follow the vowel rules

Go over each of the sounds. Say the words out loud, and have the students repeat after you. Have students call out the vowel rule for each column of the chart.

> **Teaching tip** If your students need further challenge, you could create a chart like the one on page 131 of the Student's Book. Include the vowel sound symbols in the top row of the chart, and leave the other rows blank. Then you could give students copies of the chart that they could fill in as they progress through the course. Or you could put one chart on a board in the classroom, to be filled in throughout the course.

C The letters -y- and -w- as vowels

Go over each of the sounds for the letters **-y-** and **-w-**. Say the words out loud, and have the students repeat after you. Ask your students if they can think of any other words with the letters **-y-** and **-w-** that have these sounds.

Appendix C
How Often Do the Vowel Rules Work?

These charts show how often the two pronunciation rules introduced in the book actually work for different vowel letters and letter combinations. The purpose of the charts is to encourage students to understand that it is worth their effort to learn the rules.

A The Two Vowel Rule

Ask students to each bring in one new word that fits the rule. Put the words on the board, and ask the class if they all fit the rules. You may have a few puzzling words that do not actually fit, but you can point out the vowel rule chart on page 132 of the Student's Book, which shows the percentage of time the vowels actually work. That way, the students will realize there may be exceptions, but the rule works most of the time, especially for the *strong syllable*.

B The One Vowel Rule

Ask students to each bring in one new word that fits the rule. Follow the same procedure suggested for the Two Vowel Rule above.

Appendix D
Tongue Shapes for
/t/, /d/, /s/, /z/, /θ/, /l/, and /r/

These drawings compare the mouth positions for some of the sounds practiced in the Student's Book. When students compare the sounds by looking at the differently shaped openings at the front of the mouth, they can see clearly that the airflow is different for each sound. The different configurations of the tongue shape the patterns of sound waves that the listener can hear as different speech sounds. Some of these configurations are easier to show from the side, and some are seen more clearly when viewed from the back of the mouth looking toward the front. That is why different views are shown throughout the Student's Book.

1 The /**t**/ and /**d**/ sounds are made with the same tongue position. In this position, the airflow is blocked all the way around the tooth ridge (in a horseshoe shape). The /**n**/ sound is made the same way, but the air flows out through the nose. The difference between the /**t**/ and /**d**/ sounds has to do with *voicing*, which is the presence or absence of *vibration* of the *vocal cords*. The /**t**/ is voiceless – there is no vibration of the vocal cords – while the /**d**/ is voiced – the vocal cords vibrate. This distinction is presented in the more advanced book of this series, *Clear Speech*.

2 The /**s**/ and /**z**/ sounds are made with the same tongue position. In this position, the airflow is not blocked and continues out of the mouth. To make these sounds, the tongue is v-shaped; air rushes through the narrow constriction and hits the upper front teeth, making the characteristic hissing noise. The difference between the sounds has to do with voicing. The /**s**/ is voiceless while the /**z**/ is voiced.

3 The /**θ**/ sound is made with the tongue flat, and air can flow out over it without any hissing. One way students can test this is to say the sound in a continuous stream of air and then reverse the airflow, drawing air back into the mouth. They should feel cold air flowing inward over their flat tongues.

4 The /**l**/ sound is made with the tip of the tongue touching the tooth ridge, while the rest of the tongue is kept low, allowing air to flow out on either side.

5 The /**r**/ sound is made with the tongue pulled back, and air flows over it without any stopping or hissing.

It is important to give students enough time to absorb the information they can get from these illustrations. Encourage them to quietly try out the sounds over and over, or allow them to sit and think silently while they look at the pictures. Different students will benefit differently from the pictures.

If they have already learned these sounds separately (in the units), you can have them review the entire set by asking for choral repetitions of single words, then moving on to minimal pairs of words, and then to a set for all five sounds. If students repeat words chorally many times, they will gain confidence from each other and will be able to say the sounds more strongly than if they are asked to recite individually.

Sample minimal pairs:

but	bus
made	mail
bet	bear
right	rice
boat	both

Extra Practice 1
Vowels

Alphabet vowel sounds and relative vowel sounds

The tasks in Extra Practice 1 work on developing students' mastery of the vowel distinctions. The more clearly they can pronounce these vowels in strong syllables, the more intelligible they will be.

It is most practical to teach the *alphabet vowel sounds* first, since they are a natural part of teaching the names of the alphabet letters. On the other hand, the *relative vowel sounds* are more common in English, but they tend to be more foreign for learners from other first languages.

The mouth positions for the alphabet vowels are complex, all involving a movement of the tongue and jaw, but this movement can be shown through graphic display, which is provided in parts 1 and 2. However, the relative vowel sounds are not shown graphically because the mouth positions for them are so similar to those for the alphabet vowel sounds that they are not easily distinguished visually.

Part 1 The tongue in alphabet vowel sounds

Class CD 3, Track 42

The main point about alphabet vowel sounds is that the tongue changes position upwards after the main vowel sound. The sound made during this change of position, called an *off-glide*, is brief but still important. Because such an off-glide does not exist in many other languages, it is important for students to have a lot of practice listening for it. The off-glide is shown in this book by a superscript /ʸ/ or /ʷ/ to help students remember it is part of the *vowel sound*.

Do not ask the students to repeat these sounds at this stage because vowel distinctions must basically be learned first by ear. If they speak too early, they will be hearing their own faulty acoustic model, which tends to interfere with processing the accurate model. After the students have become well accustomed to hearing the sounds, they will be better prepared to say the vowels clearly.

Part 2 The lips in alphabet vowel sounds

Class CD 3, Track 43

When the tongue shifts with an *off-glide*, the lips also change shape. This lip movement helps make the English *vowel sounds* clear.

Part 3 Practicing the vowel rules

A The Two Vowel Rule
Class CD 3, Track 44

Students can benefit by more practice applying these rules because the pronunciation of so many new words can be guessed at by this means. Previous practice was mostly with one-syllable words. In this task, students guess at and practice the pronunciation of polysyllabic words.

B The One Vowel Rule
Class CD 3, Track 45

The relative vowel sounds are the most common vowel sounds in English, and they also tend to be unusual in other languages. Therefore, extra practice with the rule is valuable.

> **Teaching tip**   To contrast the alphabet and the relative vowel sounds after you have gone through Parts 1–3, you can make a list of short words and ask students to give the symbols for the vowel sound in each word.
>
> Another approach is to ask students to bring in words from outside the classroom, place the students in small teams, and ask the teams to decide how to apply the vowel rules to the words they brought. This task can be turned into a competition by having the teams make lists together and write them on the board. They should put a vowel symbol at the top of each list. For example:
>
> | /eʸ/ | /iʸ/ | /ɑʸ/ | /oʷ/ | /uʷ/ |
> |------|------|------|------|------|
> | nails | sea | ride | soak | true |
> | date | street | file | clothes | use |

Extra Practice 2
Problem Consonants

Part 1 /v/ and /b/

Some students confuse these two sounds, pronouncing them halfway between a *stop* and a **continuant**. Pointing out the contrast between these sounds in English may help them: The **/v/** sound is a continuant and the **/b/** sound is a stop. Also, it may help to point out that the **/v/** sound is formed by the teeth touching the back of the lower lip. Some students may have a tendency to touch the teeth to the front of the lower lip, which makes the sound rather unclear.

A Listening to /v/ and /b/
Class CD 3, Track 46

Listening tasks should always precede speaking tasks. Do not ask the students to repeat the words. Let them listen only so that they can get a correct acoustic memory before they say the sounds in Task B.

B Saying /v/ and /b/

Have students pay attention to the position of their teeth and lips when repeating the two words.

C Which word do you hear?
Class CD 3, Track 47

This is the sort of practice that helps clarify the boundaries of two sounds that tend to get confused.

Audio Script

1.	vase	/veʸs/
2.	rove	/roʷv/
3.	ban	/bæn/
4.	berry	/bɛr•iʸ/
5.	vote	/voʷt/

Answer Key

1.	(vase)	base
2.	(rove)	robe
3.	van	(ban)
4.	very	(berry)
5.	(vote)	boat

Part 2 /r/ and /l/

Students from various Asian language backgrounds have difficulty distinguishing these two sounds. Because students may have been discouraged by this problem for a long time, this book does not deal with it directly in the earlier units. Instead, each sound has been practiced in contrast with another sound, in order to help students form a clear sense of the boundaries of the target sound, i.e., its difference from another sound (e.g., the final sounds in "hide" and "hire," or the distinction between "bed" and "bell"). After they have worked with those distinctions, it should be easier to deal with the **/r/** and **/l/** contrast, which may previously have been a discouraging topic. Here, the two problem sounds are brought into direct contrast.

A Listening to /r/ and /l/
Class CD 3, Track 48

If you are reading the words out loud for your students instead of playing the audio, do not exaggerate the final sounds to make your students notice the difference more easily. Instead, read the words or play the audio more than once.

C Which word do you hear?
Class CD 3, Track 49

Audio Script

1.	roar	/roʷr/	6.	rock	/rɑk/
2.	heal	/hiʸl/	7.	low	/loʷ/
3.	core	/koʷr/	8.	late	/leʸt/
4.	steel	/stiʸl/	9.	ram	/ræm/
5.	fail	/feʸl/	10.	lime	/lɑʸm/

Answer Key

	Final sound			Beginning sound	
1.	roll	(roar)	6.	lock	(rock)
2.	(heal)	hear	7.	(low)	row
3.	coal	(core)	8.	(late)	rate
4.	(steel)	steer	9.	lamb	(ram)
5.	(fail)	fair	10.	(lime)	rhyme

Part 3 /n/ and /l/

Students from some Asian languages have difficulty with this distinction, typically confusing words like "line" and "nine." If your students have no problem with these sounds, skip this topic.

🎧 A Listening to /n/ and /l/
Class CD 3, Track 50

If you are reading the words out loud for your students instead of playing the audio, do not exaggerate the final sounds to make your students notice the difference more easily. Instead, read the words or play the audio more than once.

🎧 C Which word do you hear?
Class CD 3, Track 51

Audio Script

1. pine	/paʸn/	6.	lame	/leʸm/
2. coal	/koʷl/	7.	nice	/naʸs/
3. mail	/meʸl/	8.	knife	/naʸf/
4. when	/wɛn/	9.	lease	/liʸs/
5. tool	/tuʷl/	10.	not	/nɑt/

Answer Key

Final sound		Beginning sound	
1. (pine)	pile	6. name	(lame)
2. cone	(coal)	7. (nice)	lice
3. main	(mail)	8. (knife)	life
4. (when)	well	9. niece	(lease)
5. tune	(tool)	10. (not)	lot

🎧 D The sound combinations /nd/ and /ld/
Class CD 3, Track 52

These combinations are quite difficult for students from languages that do not allow consonant clusters (two or more consonants together). Since this particular combination often carries a grammatical cue of past tense, it is important for both listening comprehension and intelligibility.

Part 4 /θ/ and /t/

The /θ/ sound (as in "think") is actually not a high priority for intelligibility, but some students are aware that they lack this sound and want help with it. The *voiced sound* /ð/ (as in "the") occurs more often in spoken English, but is relatively unimportant for intelligibility since the words it occurs in most often are *structure words* and, therefore, are typically spoken less clearly (reduced). *Voicing* distinctions are taught in the higher-level book of this series, *Clear Speech*, and there more attention can usefully be given to these two sounds.

🎧 A Listening to /θ/ and /t/
Class CD 3, Track 53

Because the /θ/ sound is relatively uncommon in the world's languages, English learners may have difficulty hearing it accurately. A common substitution learners use is the /t/ sound.

B Saying /θ/ and /t/

You may want to have students put a hand in front of their mouths so that they can feel the air flow out of their mouths when saying the word "bath."

🎧 C Which word do you hear?
Class CD 3, Track 54

Audio Script

1. bath	/bæθ/	4.	faith	/feʸθ/
2. boat	/boʷt/	5.	root	/ruʷt/
3. boot	/buʷt/	6.	math	/mæθ/

Answer Key

1. (bath)	bat
2. both	(boat)
3. booth	(boot)
4. (faith)	fate
5. Ruth	(root)
6. (math)	mat

Tests and Quizzes

In the following pages, you will find photocopiable tests and quizzes and their audio scripts and answer keys. The audio for theses items is on the Assessment CD of the Class and Assessment Audio CDs component.

Clear Listening Diagnostic Test

The purpose of this listening test is to diagnose your students' ability to understand spoken English. How your students hear English is closely related to their ability to speak clearly. Beginning the course with this diagnostic test makes it possible for both you and your students to determine what areas of listening need improvement. You may also want to give the test again later in the course so that the students will have an objective measure of their progress. Of course, you should not give the test again until the students have been thoroughly exposed to the concepts in the Student's Book and have been given adequate time to practice them.

Photocopy the test on pages 66–69 for your students. When giving the test, you can either play the audio or read the test out loud, using the audio script on pages 87–88. Each part of the test is on a separate audio track, so you can play them twice when you feel the repetition would benefit your students.

The answer key for this test is on pages 87–88. This test is worth a total of 100 points. When you score the test, be strict. The purpose is to alert your students to the need for improvement so that they will pay attention to the lessons that follow.

Clear Speaking Diagnostic Test

The purpose of this speaking test is to diagnose what parts of your students' spoken English might tend to interfere with intelligibility. Beginning the course with this diagnostic test makes it possible for both you and your students to determine what areas of speaking need improvement. You may also want to give the test again at the end of this course so that your students will have an objective measure of their progress.

Photocopy the test on page 70, and have the students record themselves speaking the dialogue in this test. Then listen to the students' recordings while looking at a copy of the dialogue. Circle each error that you hear in the dialogue. You can use this information to fill out a personal pronunciation profile form for each student. (See below.) If your students do not have access to recording equipment, they could speak the dialogue directly to you, individually.

Pronunciation Profile

The purpose of this form is to help you and your students assess their English pronunciation abilities at the beginning of the course and measure their progress at the end of the course. Photocopy the form on page 71, and fill out one form for each student.

Unit Quizzes

The purpose of these quizzes is to give you and your students an indication of their progress in listening perception. This is closely related to clarity of speaking. You may give each of the quizzes after you have finished teaching the corresponding unit, or you may combine more than one quiz if appropriate.

Photocopy the quizzes on pages 72–86 for your students. When giving a quiz, you can either play the audio or read the quiz out loud, using the audio script on pages 89–96. To adjust to the level of your students, read slower or quicker depending on their ability to process what they hear. If you think your students need more time to process what is on the audio, you can pause the audio after each item to give your students more time to answer. Each task on a quiz is on a separate audio track, so you can play them twice when you feel the repetition would benefit your students.

The answer keys for these quizzes are on pages 89–96. Each quiz is worth a total of 20 points. If you need or want to give your students a grade, you can add up the scores for each quiz. Otherwise, you can simply mark the errors so that the students can see them.

Clear Listening Diagnostic Test

Name _____

Date _____ [____ / 100 points]

◎ Part 1 – Vowels

Listen. You will hear either word *a* or word *b*. Circle the letter of the word you hear. The first one is done as an example.

1. a. main
   b. man

2. a. wheel
   b. well

3. a. ice
   b. is

4. a. hope
   b. hop

5. a. cut
   b. cute

6. a. soak
   b. sock

7. a. luck
   b. lock

8. a. us
   b. use

9. a. rain
   b. ran

10. a. meat
    b. met

11. a. grace
    b. grass

[_____ / 10 points]

Photocopiable   © Cambridge University Press 2012

◎ Part 2 – Consonants

Listen. You will hear either word *a* or word *b*. Circle the letter of the word you hear. The first one is done as an example.

1. (a.) has
   b. had
2. a. cake
   b. cakes
3. a. city
   b. cities
4. a. coal
   b. cold
5. a. feel
   b. feed
6. a. car
   b. card
7. a. spell
   b. spelled
8. a. where
   b. what
9. a. supermarket
   b. supermarkets
10. a. well
    b. when
11. a. mass
    b. math

[_____ / 10 points]

◎ Part 3 – Number of syllables

Listen to the words. Write the number of syllables you hear in each word. The first one is done as an example.

1. easy   __2__
2. opened   _____
3. eleven   _____
4. clothes   _____
5. Wednesday   _____
6. called   _____

[_____ / 10 points]

◎ Part 4 – Strong syllables

Listen. In each word, one syllable is stronger than the others. Underline the strong syllable you hear. The first one is done as an example.

1. comp<u>u</u>ter
2. coffee
3. elephant
4. ticket
5. television
6. sesame

7. America
8. information
9. Canada
10. syllable
11. practical

[_____ / 10 points]

◎ Part 5 – Weak syllables

Listen. In each word, there is one weak vowel. Draw a line through the weak vowel letter. The first one is done as an example.

1. sal~~a~~d
2. pencil
3. salmon
4. China
5. Japan
6. tomato

7. sofa
8. jacket
9. glasses
10. raisin
11. Brazil

[_____ / 10 points]

◎ Part 6 – The most important word

Listen. You will hear each dialogue two times. In each sentence of the dialogue, one word is the most important. Underline the most important word you hear in each sentence. The first one is done as an example.

1. A: What's the <u>matter</u>?
   B: I lost my <u>keys</u>.
2. A: The world is flat.
   B: No, it's round.
3. A: I want a cheese sandwich.
   B: I want a cup of soup.
4. A: I lost my books.
   B: Which books?
5. A: Where are my glasses?
   B: Under the table.
6. A: I'd like some tea.
   B: Do you want lemon in your tea?

[_____ / 20 points]

Photocopiable

◎ Part 7 – Weak words

Listen. You will hear each sentence two times. One word is missing in each sentence. Write the missing word you hear on the blank line. The first one is done as an example.

1. I'd like a cup ___of___ coffee, please.

2. I'd like a salad _____ pie, please.

3. We need ten _____ them.

4. She wants _____ burger.

5. Joe wants tea _____ cake.

6. I'll have _____ ham sandwich.

[_____ / 10 points]

◎ Part 8 – Numbers

Listen. You will hear a sentence two times. Circle the correct number you hear in each sentence. The first one is done as an example.

1. They have **15** / **50** books.

2. They need **14** / **40** pencils.

3. The party is on March **5th** / **6th**.

4. They need **25** / **29** more books.

5. There are **7** / **70** students.

6. The sale begins on October **4th** / **5th**.

7. The table is **13** / **30** years old.

8. She was born in **1918** / **1980**.

9. The shop opened in **1916** / **1960**.

10. His phone number is **555-1658** / **555-1698**.

11. Her phone number is **212-555-4814** / **202-555-4814**.

[_____ / 20 points]

Clear Speaking Diagnostic Test

Practice saying this dialogue until you are comfortable with it. Then record it or read it out loud to your teacher, speaking as naturally as possible.

Shopping for a Birthday Gift

Clerk: [1] Can I help you?

Customer: [2] I'm looking for a gift.

Clerk: [3] What kind of gift?

Customer: [4] A birthday gift.

Clerk: [5] Who is this gift for?

Customer: [6] My sister.

Clerk: [7] Excuse me, but how old is your sister?

Customer: [8] She's going to be seven years old.

Clerk: [9] Oh, I see. And what does she like?

Customer: [10] She likes things that are pink.

Clerk: [11] How about this pink backpack?

Customer: [12] Well, I don't know.

Clerk: [13] Maybe she'd like pink shoes or a dress.

Customer: [14] I'm afraid she already has pink shoes.

Clerk: [15] Here's a pink dress. What size is she?

Customer: [16] Size seven.

Clerk: [17] Do you think she'll like it?

Customer: [18] Oh yes! She'll say it's a dream dress!

Pronunciation Profile

Name _____

Date _____

The checked areas need improvement.

1 Rhythm and word stress   **List of errors**

___ Using the correct number of syllables   _____

___ Stressing the correct syllable   _____

___ Lengthening the vowel in a stressed syllable _____

___ Using schwa in reduced syllables   _____

___ Linking words   _____

2 Emphasis and thought groups

___ Emphasizing the most important words   _____

___ De-emphasizing less important words   _____

3 Sounds

___ Using a clear vowel in the strong syllable _____

___ Using correct consonant sounds at
     the end of words   _____

Unit 1 Quiz

Name _____

Date _____   [____ / 20 points]

◎ **A** Listen to the words. Do you hear the /eʸ/ sound as in the word "cake"?
Mark *Yes* or *No* for each word.

    Yes   **No**

1. _____   _____
2. _____   _____
3. _____   _____
4. _____   _____

[_____ / 4 points]

◎ **B** Listen to the words. Do you hear the /iʸ/ sound as in the word "tea"?
Mark *Yes* or *No* for each word.

    Yes   **No**

1. _____   _____
2. _____   _____
3. _____   _____
4. _____   _____

[_____ / 4 points]

◎ **C** Listen to the words. Do you hear the /aʸ/ sound as in the word "ice"?
Mark *Yes* or *No* for each word.

    Yes   **No**

1. _____   _____
2. _____   _____
3. _____   _____
4. _____   _____

[_____ / 4 points]

◎ **D** Listen to the words. Do you hear the /oʷ/ sound as in the word "cone"?
Mark *Yes* or *No* for each word.

    Yes   **No**

1. _____   _____
2. _____   _____
3. _____   _____
4. _____   _____

[_____ / 4 points]

◎ **E** Listen to the words. Do you hear the /uʷ/ sound as in the word "cube"?
Mark *Yes* or *No* for each word.

    Yes   **No**

1. _____   _____
2. _____   _____
3. _____   _____
4. _____   _____

[_____ / 4 points]

Unit 2 Quiz

Name _____

Date _____   [____ / 20 points]

◎ **A** Listen. In each word, underline the letter that says its alphabet name.

1. name	6. train
2. cream	7. these
3. pie	8. fruit
4. home	9. Joan
5. rule	10. time

[_____ / 10 points]

◎ **B** Listen. Circle the word you hear.

1. meat	mate	mute
2. eat	ate	oat
3. coat	cute	kite
4. mine	moan	mean
5. line	lone	lean

[_____ / 10 points]

Unit 3 Quiz

Name _____

Date _____

[___ / 20 points]

◎ **A** Listen. You will hear a word two times. Write the number of syllables you hear in each word.

1. _____
2. _____
3. _____
4. _____
5. _____

[_____ / 10 points]

◎ **B** Listen. Circle the word you hear.

1. seven   seventy
2. sit   city
3. closed   close it
4. nine   ninety
5. salt   salad
6. ease   easy
7. a store   store
8. blow   below
9. repeat   repeated
10. planned   planet

[_____ / 10 points]

Unit 4 Quiz

Name _____

Date _____   [____ / 20 points]

◎ **A** Listen. You will hear a set of three words two times. One word is different. Mark it.

	X	Y	Z
1.	_____	_____	_____
2.	_____	_____	_____
3.	_____	_____	_____
4.	_____	_____	_____
5.	_____	_____	_____

[_____ / 10 points]

◎ **B** Listen. You will hear either sentence *a* or sentence *b* two times. Circle the letter of the sentence you hear.

1. a. Did you say "pine"?
   b. Did you say "pin"?

2. a. What does "cube" mean?
   b. What does "cub" mean?

3. a. I took the wrong road.
   b. I took the wrong rod.

4. a. How do you spell "wheel"?
   b. How do you spell "well"?

5. a. Is that a shack?
   b. Is that a shake?

[_____ / 10 points]

Unit 5 Quiz

Name _____

Date _____

[___ / 20 points]

◎ **A** Listen to the words. Underline the strong syllable you hear in each word.

1. Chicago
2. Toronto
3. freezer
4. agree
5. creamy
6. telephone
7. complain
8. open
9. newspaper
10. arrive

[_____ / 10 points]

◎ **B** Listen. You will hear a word two times. Write the number of syllables you hear in each word.

1. _____
2. _____
3. _____
4. _____
5. _____

[_____ / 10 points]

Unit 6 Quiz

Name _____

Date _____   [___ / 20 points]

◎ **A** Listen. You will hear each word two times. Draw a line through the weak vowel in each word.

1. chicken

2. lemon

3. butter

4. alarm

5. salad

[_____ / 10 points]

◎ **B** Listen. You will hear each sentence two times. Write the missing word you hear on the blank line.

1. They drink coffee _____ tea.

2. Two slices _____ cake, please.

3. Coffee _____ cream, please.

4. She wants _____ bowl of spaghetti.

5. What kind _____ soup do you want?

[_____ / 10 points]

Unit 7 Quiz

Name _____

Date _____

[____ / 20 points]

◎ **A** Listen. You will hear this dialogue two times. Underline the most important word you hear in each sentence.

A: ¹ What's the matter?

B: ² I lost my book.

A: ³ Which book?

B: ⁴ My English book.

A: ⁵ When did you have it?

B: ⁶ Yesterday morning.

A: ⁷ Where were you?

B: ⁸ On the train.

A: ⁹ I hope you find it.

B: ¹⁰ Me, too!

[____ / 10 points]

◎ **B** Listen. You will hear each sentence two times. Underline the most important word you hear in the sentence. Then circle the letter of the best question to follow the sentence.

1. I wanted a cup of tea.
   a. Not coffee?
   b. Not a pot?

2. I'm going to meet my father at one.
   a. Not your mother?
   b. Not at two?

3. We need three plates.
   a. Not bowls?
   b. Not four?

4. He lost his black dog!
   a. Oh, not his cat?
   b. Oh, not the brown one?

5. This is chocolate pie!
   a. Did you want lemon?
   b. Did you want cake?

[____ / 10 points]

Unit 8 Quiz

Name _____

Date _____   [____ / 20 points]

◎ **A** Listen. You will hear a set of three words two times. One word is different. Mark it.

X	Y	Z
1. _____	_____	_____
2. _____	_____	_____
3. _____	_____	_____
4. _____	_____	_____
5. _____	_____	_____

[_____ / 10 points]

◎ **B** Listen. You will hear a sentence two times. Mark *Singular* (one thing) or *Plural* (more than one thing) for the last word you hear in each sentence.

Singular	Plural
1. _____	_____
2. _____	_____
3. _____	_____
4. _____	_____
5. _____	_____

[_____ / 10 points]

Unit 9 Quiz

Name _____

Date _____

[____ / 20 points]

A Listen. Circle the word you hear.

1. food   fool
2. bed   bell
3. paid   pail
4. feed   feel
5. road   roll
6. wade   whale
7. tide   tile
8. fade   fail
9. made   mail
10. raid   rail

[_____ / 10 points]

B Listen. You will hear a sentence two times. Mark *Present* or *Future* for the sentence you hear.

	Present	**Future**
1.	_____	_____
2.	_____	_____
3.	_____	_____
4.	_____	_____
5.	_____	_____

[_____ / 10 points]

   Photocopiable

Unit 10 Quiz

Name _____

Date _____   [____ / 20 points]

A Listen. Circle the word you hear.

1. called   call
2. cold   coal
3. sailed   sail
4. hold   hole
5. gold   goal
6. field   feel
7. made   mail
8. filled   fill
9. pulled   pull
10. bold   bowl

[_____ / 10 points]

B Listen. You will hear a sentence two times. Mark *Present* or *Past* for the sentence you hear.

	Present	**Past**
1.	_____	_____
2.	_____	_____
3.	_____	_____
4.	_____	_____
5.	_____	_____

[_____ / 10 points]

Unit 11 Quiz

Name _____

Date _____

[____ / 20 points]

A Listen. You will hear a set of three words two times. One word is different. Mark it.

	X	Y	Z
1.	_____	_____	_____
2.	_____	_____	_____
3.	_____	_____	_____
4.	_____	_____	_____
5.	_____	_____	_____

[_____ / 10 points]

B Listen. You will hear a question two times. Circle the letter of the best answer to the question you hear.

1. a. To fix.
   b. The past of "repair."

2. a. W - H - A - T.
   b. W - H - E - R - E.

3. a. F - E - A - R.
   b. F - E - A - R - E - D.

4. a. The noise of a lion.
   b. The past of "roar."

5. a. P - A - I - D.
   b. P - A - I - R.

[_____ / 10 points]

Unit 12 Quiz

◎ **A** Listen to the words. Do you hear a final /s/ or /z/ sound? Mark *Yes* or *No* for each word.

	Yes	No
1.	_____	_____
2.	_____	_____
3.	_____	_____
4.	_____	_____
5.	_____	_____
6.	_____	_____
7.	_____	_____
8.	_____	_____
9.	_____	_____
10.	_____	_____

[____ / 10 points]

◎ **B** Listen. You will hear a sentence two times. Do you hear a /s/ or /z/ sound in the sentence? Mark *Yes* or *No*.

	Yes	No
1.	_____	_____
2.	_____	_____
3.	_____	_____
4.	_____	_____
5.	_____	_____

[____ / 10 points]

Unit 13 Quiz

Name _____

Date _____

[____ / 20 points]

◎ **A** Listen. Circle the number you hear.

1. 30   13
2. 20   12
3. 60   16
4. 93   96
5. 70   17
6. 40   14
7. 2080   2018
8. 1990   1919
9. 2035   2039
10. 1950   1915

[_____ / 10 points]

◎ **B** Listen. You will hear this dialogue two times. Write the missing numbers you hear in the information clerk's lines. Don't spell out the numbers.

Customer:	Excuse me, where is the bookstore?
Information Clerk:	It's at _____ A.
Customer:	Thanks. What's the phone number?
Information Clerk:	It's 555-1 _____ 97.
Customer:	Thanks. And where is the café?
Information Clerk:	It's at _____ B.
Customer:	And what time do they open?
Information Clerk:	They open at _____.
Customer:	And what time do they close?
Information Clerk:	At _____ on weeknights.

[_____ / 10 points]

Unit 14 Quiz

Name _____

Date _____   [___ / 20 points]

◎ **A** Listen. You will hear a set of three words two times. One word is different. Mark it.

	X	Y	Z
1.	_____	_____	_____
2.	_____	_____	_____
3.	_____	_____	_____
4.	_____	_____	_____
5.	_____	_____	_____

[_____ / 10 points]

◎ **B** Listen. You will hear a sentence two times. Circle the correct word you hear in each sentence.

1. We **own / owned** a house.
2. They **spell / spelled** all the words.
3. Will you go on the **train / trail?**
4. How do you spell **"coal" / "cold"**?
5. What does **"when" / "well"** mean?

[_____ / 10 points]

Unit 15 Quiz

Name _____

Date _____

[____ / 20 points]

◎ **A** Listen. You will hear a set of three words two times. One word is different. Mark it.

	X	Y	Z
1.	_____	_____	_____
2.	_____	_____	_____
3.	_____	_____	_____
4.	_____	_____	_____
5.	_____	_____	_____

[_____ / 10 points]

◎ **B** Listen. You will hear a question two times. Circle the letter of the best answer to the question you hear.

1. a. B - A - T - H.
   b. B - A - S - S.

2. a. P - A - T.
   b. P - A - T - H.

3. a. Work with numbers.
   b. A small rug.

4. a. To get clean.
   b. To play baseball.

5. a. Two things. Not just one of them.
   b. A small ship.

[_____ / 10 points]

Photocopiable

Test and Quizzes
Audio Scripts and Answer Keys

If you are reading the scripts for your students instead of playing the audio, please see the instructions in bold and in parentheses before each task.

Clear Listening Diagnostic Test

Part 1 – Vowels

⊚ **Assessment CD, Track 2**

(Teacher: You might want to play or read each word twice. Don't read the circled letters.)

Listen. You will hear either word *a* or word *b*. Circle the letter of the word you hear. The first one is done as an example.

1. (a.) main
2. (a.) wheel
3. (b.) is
4. (a.) hope
5. (a.) cut
6. (b.) sock
7. (a.) luck
8. (a.) us
9. (b.) ran
10. (b.) met
11. (a.) grace

Part 2 – Consonants

⊚ **Assessment CD, Track 3**

(Teacher: You might want to play or read each word twice. Don't read the circled letters.)

Listen. You will hear either word *a* or word *b*. Circle the letter of the word you hear. The first one is done as an example.

1. (a.) has
2. (b.) cakes
3. (b.) cities
4. (b.) cold
5. (a.) feel
6. (b.) card
7. (b.) spelled
8. (a.) where
9. (b.) supermarkets
10. (a.) well
11. (a.) mass

Part 3 – Number of syllables

⊚ **Assessment CD, Track 4**

(Teacher: You might want to play or read each word twice. Don't read the numbers to their right.)

Listen to the words. Write the number of syllables you hear in each word. The first one is done as an example.

1. ea•sy   _2_
2. o•pened   _2_
3. e•lev•en   _3_
4. clothes   _1_
5. Wednes•day   _2_
6. called   _1_

Part 4 – Strong syllables

⊚ **Assessment CD, Track 5**

(Teacher: You might want to play or read each word twice. Make sure to stress the underlined syllables.)

Listen. In each word, one syllable is stronger than the others. Underline the strong syllable you hear. The first one is done as an example.

1. com<u>pu</u>ter
2. <u>cof</u>fee
3. <u>el</u>ephant
4. <u>tick</u>et
5. <u>tel</u>evision
6. <u>ses</u>ame
7. A<u>mer</u>ica
8. infor<u>ma</u>tion
9. <u>Can</u>ada
10. <u>syl</u>lable
11. <u>prac</u>tical

Part 5 – Weak syllables

Assessment CD, Track 6

(Teacher: You might want to play or read each word twice. Be careful not to emphasize the reduced vowels.)

Listen. In each word, there is one weak vowel. Draw a line through the weak vowel letter. The first one is done as an example.

1. sal~a~d
2. penc~i~l
3. salm~o~n
4. Chin~a~
5. J~a~pan
6. t~o~mato
7. sof~a~
8. jack~e~t
9. glass~e~s
10. rais~i~n
11. Br~a~zil

Part 6 – The most important word

Assessment CD, Track 7

(Teacher: Play or read each dialogue twice. Make sure to emphasize the underlined words.)

Listen. You will hear each dialogue two times. In each sentence of the dialogue, one word is the most important. Underline the most important word you hear in each sentence. The first one is done as an example.

1. A: What's the <u>matter</u>?
   B: I lost my <u>keys</u>.

2. A: The world is <u>flat</u>.
   B: No, it's <u>round</u>.

3. A: I want a <u>cheese</u> sandwich.
   B: I want a cup of <u>soup</u>.

4. A: I lost my <u>books</u>.
   B: <u>Which</u> books?

5. A: Where are my <u>glasses</u>?
   B: Under the <u>table</u>.

6. A: I'd like some <u>tea</u>.
   B: Do you want <u>lemon</u> in your tea?

Part 7 – Weak words

Assessment CD, Track 8

(Teacher: Play or read each sentence twice. Make sure to reduce *a*, *and*, and *of*.)

Listen. You will hear each sentence two times. One word is missing in each sentence. Write the missing word you hear on the blank line. The first one is done as an example.

1. I'd like a cup <u>of</u> coffee, please.
2. I'd like a salad <u>and</u> pie, please.
3. We need ten <u>of</u> them.
4. She wants <u>a</u> burger.
5. Joe wants tea <u>and</u> cake.
6. I'll have <u>a</u> ham sandwich.

Part 8 – Numbers

Assessment CD, Track 9

(Teacher: Play or read each sentence twice.)

Listen. You will hear a sentence two times. Circle the correct number you hear in each sentence. The first one is done as an example.

1. They have ⑮ books.
2. They need ㊵ pencils.
3. The party is on March ⑤th.
4. They need ㉕ more books.
5. There are ⑦ students.
6. The sale begins on October ④th.
7. The table is ㉚ years old.
8. She was born in ⑲⑱.
9. The shop opened in ⑲⑥⓪.
10. His phone number is ⑤⑤⑤-①⑥⑤⑧.
11. Her phone number is ②⓪②-⑤⑤⑤-④⑧①④.

Unit 1 Quiz

A

🎧 Assessment CD, Track 10

(Teacher: You might want to play or read each word twice. Don't read the columns to their right.)

Listen to the words. Do you hear the /e^y/ sound as in the word "cake"? Mark *Yes* or *No* for each word.

	Yes	No
1. take	✓	
2. show		✓
3. name	✓	
4. low		✓

B

🎧 Assessment CD, Track 11

(Teacher: You might want to play or read each word twice. Don't read the columns to their right.)

Listen to the words. Do you hear the /i^y/ sound as in the word "tea"? Mark *Yes* or *No* for each word.

	Yes	No
1. pie		✓
2. see	✓	
3. cream	✓	
4. fine		✓

C

🎧 Assessment CD, Track 12

(Teacher: You might want to play or read each word twice. Don't read the columns to their right.)

Listen to the words. Do you hear the /a^y/ sound as in the word "ice"? Mark *Yes* or *No* for each word.

	Yes	No
1. fries	✓	
2. sea		✓
3. hi	✓	
4. my	✓	

D

🎧 Assessment CD, Track 13

(Teacher: You might want to play or read each word twice. Don't read the columns to their right.)

Listen to the words. Do you hear the /o^w/ sound as in the word "cone"? Mark *Yes* or *No* for each word.

	Yes	No
1. home	✓	
2. slow	✓	
3. these		✓
4. soap	✓	

E

🎧 Assessment CD, Track 14

(Teacher: You might want to play or read each word twice. Don't read the columns to their right.)

Listen to the words. Do you hear the /u^w/ sound as in the word "cube"? Mark *Yes* or *No* for each word.

	Yes	No
1. suit	✓	
2. boat		✓
3. true	✓	
4. same		✓

Unit 2 Quiz

A

🎧 Assessment CD, Track 15

(Teacher: You might want to play or read each word twice.)

Listen. In each word, underline the letter that says its alphabet name.

1. n<u>a</u>me
2. cr<u>ea</u>m
3. p<u>ie</u>
4. h<u>o</u>me
5. r<u>u</u>le
6. tr<u>ai</u>n
7. th<u>e</u>se
8. fr<u>ui</u>t
9. J<u>oa</u>n
10. t<u>i</u>me

B

🎧 Assessment CD, Track 16

(Teacher: You might want to play or read each word twice.)

Listen. Circle the word you hear.

1. (mute)
2. (ate)
3. (coat)
4. (mine)
5. (lean)

Unit 3 Quiz

A

◎ **Assessment CD, Track 17**

(Teacher: Play or read each word twice. Don't read the number of syllables to their right.)

Listen. You will hear a word two times. Write the number of syllables you hear in each word.

1. sev•en   __2__
2. close   __1__
3. thir•ty   __2__
4. hou•ses   __2__
5. pain•ted   __2__

B

◎ **Assessment CD, Track 18**

(Teacher: You might want to play or read each word twice.)

Listen. Circle the word you hear.

1. (seventy)
2. (sit)
3. (closed)
4. (ninety)
5. (salad)
6. (ease)
7. (store)
8. (blow)
9. (repeated)
10. (planned)

Unit 4 Quiz

A

◎ **Assessment CD, Track 19**

(Teacher: Play or read each set of words twice. Don't read the columns to their right.)

Listen. You will hear a set of three words two times. One word is different. Mark it.

	X	Y	Z
1. late, late, let			✓
2. sit, sit, site			✓
3. cute, cut, cute		✓	
4. ten, teen, teen	✓		
5. hope, hop, hope		✓	

B

◎ **Assessment CD, Track 20**

(Teacher: Play or read each sentence twice. Don't read the circled letters.)

Listen. You will hear either sentence *a* or sentence *b* two times. Circle the letter of the sentence you hear.

1. (b.) Did you say "pin"?
2. (b.) What does "cub" mean?
3. (a.) I took the wrong road.
4. (b.) How do you spell "well"?
5. (a.) Is that a shack?

Unit 5 Quiz

A

Assessment CD, Track 21

(Teacher: You might want to play or read each word twice. Make sure to stress the underlined syllables.)

Listen to the words. Underline the strong syllable you hear in each word.

1. Chi<u>ca</u>go
2. To<u>ron</u>to
3. <u>free</u>zer
4. a<u>gree</u>
5. <u>cream</u>y
6. <u>tel</u>ephone
7. com<u>plain</u>
8. <u>open</u>
9. <u>news</u>paper
10. ar<u>rive</u>

B

Assessment CD, Track 22

(Teacher: Play or read each word twice. Don't read the number of syllables to their right.)

Listen. You will hear a word two times. Write the number of syllables you hear in each word.

1. blan•ket   2
2. el•e•phant   3
3. news•pa•per   3
4. tel•e•vis•ion   4
5. trained   1

Unit 6 Quiz

A

Assessment CD, Track 23

(Teacher: Play or read each word twice. Make sure to reduce the weak vowels.)

Listen. You will hear each word two times. Draw a line through the weak vowel in each word.

1. chick~~e~~n
2. lem~~o~~n
3. butt~~e~~r
4. ~~a~~larm
5. sal~~a~~d

B

Assessment CD, Track 24

(Teacher: Play or read each sentence twice. Don't emphasize *a*, *and*, or *of*.)

Listen. You will hear each sentence two times. Write the missing word you hear on the blank line.

1. They drink coffee <u>and</u> tea.
2. Two slices <u>of</u> cake, please.
3. Coffee <u>and</u> cream, please.
4. She wants <u>a</u> bowl of spaghetti.
5. What kind <u>of</u> soup do you want?

Unit 7 Quiz

A

⊚ Assessment CD, Track 25

(Teacher: Play or read the dialogue twice. Make sure to emphasize the underlined words.)

Listen. You will hear this dialogue two times. Underline the most important word you hear in each sentence.

A: ¹ What's the <u>matter</u>?

B: ² I lost my <u>book</u>.

A: ³ <u>Which</u> book?

B: ⁴ My <u>English</u> book.

A: ⁵ When did you <u>have</u> it?

B: ⁶ Yesterday <u>morning</u>.

A: ⁷ Where <u>were</u> you?

B: ⁸ On the <u>train</u>.

A: ⁹ I hope you <u>find</u> it.

B: ¹⁰ Me, <u>too</u>!

B

⊚ Assessment CD, Track 26

(Teacher: Play or read each sentence twice. Don't read the questions in the right column.)

Listen. You will hear each sentence two times. Underline the most important word you hear in the sentence.
Then circle the letter of the best question to follow the sentence.

1. I wanted a <u>cup</u> of tea.   (b.) Not a pot?

2. I'm going to meet my <u>father</u> at one.   (a.) Not your mother?

3. We need three <u>plates</u>.   (a.) Not bowls?

4. He lost his black <u>dog</u>!   (a.) Oh, not his cat?

5. This is chocolate <u>pie</u>!   (b.) Did you want cake?

Unit 8 Quiz

A

⊚ Assessment CD, Track 27

(Teacher: Play or read each set of words twice. Don't read the columns to their right.)

Listen. You will hear a set of three words two times. One word is different. Mark it.

	X	Y	Z
1. had, had, has			✓
2. rise, ride, ride	✓		
3. night, night, nice			✓
4. ticket, tickets, ticket		✓	
5. it, it, is			✓

B

⊚ Assessment CD, Track 28

(Teacher: Play or read each sentence twice. Don't read the columns to their right.)

Listen. You will hear a sentence two times. Mark *Singular* (one thing) or *Plural* (more than one thing) for the last word you hear in each sentence.

	Singular	Plural
1. They sell coats.		✓
2. She likes hats.		✓
3. They bought a postcard.	✓	
4. How do you spell "cakes"?		✓
5. Did you say "jacket"?	✓	

Unit 9 Quiz

A

Assessment CD, Track 29

(Teacher: You might want to play or read each word twice.)

Listen. Circle the word you hear.

1. (fool)
2. (bed)
3. (pail)
4. (feed)
5. (roll)
6. (wade)
7. (tide)
8. (fail)
9. (mail)
10. (raid)

B

Assessment CD, Track 30

(Teacher: Play or read each sentence twice. Don't read the columns to their right.)

Listen. You will hear a sentence two times. Mark *Present* or *Future* for the sentence you hear.

	Present	Future
1. I'll drive to work.		✓
2. We'll ask questions.		✓
3. I make breakfast.	✓	
4. I'll write books.		✓
5. They work hard.	✓	

Unit 10 Quiz

A

Assessment CD, Track 31

(Teacher: You might want to play or read each word twice.)

Listen. Circle the word you hear.

1. (call)
2. (cold)
3. (sailed)
4. (hold)
5. (goal)
6. (field)
7. (mail)
8. (fill)
9. (pull)
10. (bold)

B

Assessment CD, Track 32

(Teacher: Play or read each sentence twice. Don't read the columns to their right.)

Listen. You will hear a sentence two times. Mark *Present* or *Past* for the sentence you hear.

	Present	Past
1. I call my friend.	✓	
2. People mailed letters.		✓
3. We spelled all the words.		✓
4. They pull all the ropes.	✓	
5. We sailed our boats.		✓

Unit 11 Quiz

A

Assessment CD, Track 33

(Teacher: Play or read each set of words twice. Don't read the columns to their right.)

Listen. You will hear a set of three words two times. One word is different. Mark it.

	X	Y	Z
1. are, are, art			✓
2. fear, feed, feed	✓		
3. neat, neat, near			✓
4. tired, tire, tired		✓	
5. scored, score, score	✓		

B

Assessment CD, Track 34

(Teacher: Play or read each question twice. Don't read the answers in the column on the right.)

Listen. You will hear a question two times. Circle the letter of the best answer to the question you hear.

1. What does "repaired" mean?   (b.) The past of "repair."
2. How do you spell "where"?   (b.) W-H-E-R-E.
3. How do you spell "fear"?   (a.) F-E-A-R.
4. What does "roar" mean?   (a.) The noise of a lion.
5. How do you spell "paid"?   (a.) P-A-I-D.

Unit 12 Quiz

A

Assessment CD, Track 35

(Teacher: You might want to play or read each word twice. Don't read the columns to their right.)

Listen to the words. Do you hear a final /s/ or /z/ sound? Mark *Yes* or *No* for each word.

	Yes	No
1. parks	✓	
2. fries	✓	
3. map		✓
4. theater		✓
5. toys	✓	
6. hotels	✓	
7. laundromat		✓
8. banks	✓	
9. hospitals	✓	
10. alley		✓

B

Assessment CD, Track 36

(Teacher: Play or read each sentence twice. Don't read the columns to their right.)

Listen. You will hear a sentence two times. Do you hear a /s/ or /z/ sound in the sentence? Mark *Yes* or *No*.

	Yes	No
1. The bus is full.	✓	
2. Will the office open today?	✓	
3. Can we complete all the work in time?		✓
4. We're never late to work.		✓
5. What excuse are you giving?	✓	

Unit 13 Quiz

A

Assessment CD, Track 37

(Teacher: You might want to play or read each number twice.)

Listen. Circle the number you hear.

1. (30)
2. (20)
3. (16)
4. (96)
5. (17)
6. (40)
7. (2018)
8. (1990)
9. (2035)
10. (1915)

B

Assessment CD, Track 38

(Teacher: Play or read the dialogue twice. Don't emphasize the numbers, but read them clearly.)

Listen. You will hear this dialogue two times. Write the missing numbers you hear in the information clerk's lines. Don't spell out the numbers.

Customer:	Excuse me, where is the bookstore?
Information Clerk:	It's at 30 A.
Customer:	Thanks. What's the phone number?
Information Clerk:	It's 555-1697.
Customer:	Thanks. And where is the café?
Information Clerk:	It's at 19 B.
Customer:	And what time do they open?
Information Clerk:	They open at 10.
Customer:	And what time do they close?
Information Clerk:	At 8 on weeknights.

Unit 14 Quiz

A

Assessment CD, Track 39

(Teacher: Play or read each set of words twice. Don't read the columns to their right.)

Listen. You will hear a set of three words two times. One word is different. Mark it.

	X	Y	Z
1. mail, mail, main			✓
2. filled, fill, fill	✓		
3. ten, ten, tend			✓
4. mile, mild, mile		✓	
5. plan, plan, planned			✓

B

Assessment CD, Track 40

(Teacher: Play or read each sentence twice.)

Listen. You will hear a sentence two times.
Circle the correct word you hear in each sentence.

1. We (owned) a house.
2. They (spelled) all the words.
3. Will you go on the (train)?
4. How do you spell ("coal")?
5. What does ("when") mean?

Unit 15 Quiz

A

Assessment CD, Track 41

**(Teacher: Play or read each set of words twice.
Don't read the columns to their right.)**
Listen. You will hear a set of three words two times.
One word is different. Mark it.

	X	Y	Z
1. mass, math, mass		✓	
2. boat, both, both	✓		
3. mouth, mouth, mouse			✓
4. with, wit, wit	✓		
5. faith, faith, face			✓

B

Assessment CD, Track 42

**(Teacher: Play or read each question twice.
Don't read the answers in the column on the right.)**
Listen. You will hear a question two times. Circle the
letter of the best answer to the question you hear.

1. How do you spell "bass"?   (b.) B-A-S-S.
2. How do you spell "pat"?   (a.) P-A-T.
3. What does "mat" mean?   (b.) A small rug.
4. What's a bath for?   (a.) To get clean.
5. What does "both" mean?   (a.) Two things. Not
   just one of them.

Glossary

alphabet vowel sound Alphabet vowel sounds are pronounced like the names of the English vowel letters -a-, -e-, -i-, -o-, and -u-. The alphabet vowel sounds are /eʸ/ (cake), /iʸ/ (tea), /ɑʸ/ (ice), /oʷ/ (cone), /uʷ/ (blue). (compare *relative vowel sound*)

combination sound A combination sound is made by combining a stop sound with a continuant. Examples: /tʃ/ (cheap), /dʒ/ (junk)

consonant sound A consonant sound is made by bringing the tongue close enough to some part of the mouth to produce pressure. (compare *vowel sound*) Examples: /s/ (sea), /t/ (too), /l/ (low)

content word Content words – like nouns, verbs, and adjectives – carry the most information in a sentence and usually can bring a picture to mind. (compare *structure word*) Examples: "bike," "run," "green"

continuant sound A continuant sound is made by leaving an opening for air to flow from the mouth or the nose. A continuant sound can last as long as the speaker has air to continue it. (compare *stop sound*) Examples: /l/ (tell), /n/ (tan), /f/ (safe), /θ/ (bath)

contraction Auxiliary verbs and the word "not" are often shortened and connected to the word that comes before them. This shortened form is called a "contraction." Examples: "I'll," "can't"

contrast The vowel in the most important syllable in a word (the stressed syllable) is made extra long and extra clear, while other syllables are pronounced less clearly. This contrast in length and clarity makes the important syllable easier to hear. The primary stress of the most important word in a thought group (the focus word) is made extra long and clear and is said with a pitch change. This also creates a contrast, so that the important word can be noticed more easily

emphasis Emphasis is the way native English speakers highlight the most important words in what they say (the focus words) to show a contrast with less important words. Emphasis is added to a word by making the stressed syllable extra long and clear and adding a pitch change.
Example:

We're all waiting for you.

focus word A focus word is the most important word in a thought group. Focus words are emphasized with a pitch change and a long, clear vowel in the stressed syllable to help the listener notice them.
Example:

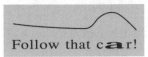

Follow that car!

linking This occurs when a final sound continues, so as to link with the beginning sound of the next word. This is done to keep a word group together.

most important word Each word group (or "thought group") has one important word (the "focus word").

off-glide After the main sound of the alphabet vowel sounds, the tongue moves up to provide an after-sound (e.g., the second part of /eʸ/). It is shown in the book by the little superscript /ʸ/ or /ʷ/.

peak vowel This is the clear vowel sound in a strong syllable. This must be pronounced extra clear.

pitch pattern This is the musical change in the voice, up or down, that helps the listener notice the important words (focus words).
Example:

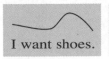

I want shoes.   New shoes.

relative vowel sound Relative vowel sounds are the vowel pronunciations that do not sound like the names of the vowel letters. (compare *alphabet vowel sounds*)
Examples: /æ/ (pan), /ɛ/ (ten), /ɪ/ (is), /ɑ/ (top), /ʌ/ (cut)

rhythm Rhythm is the pattern of long and short syllables.

□□⬜   □ □ ⬜

Example: absolute   Have some fruit.

schwa Schwa (/ə/) is the reduced vowel sound. It is very short and very unclear. By reducing less important syllables in a word to schwa, the most important syllable (the stressed syllable) is made more noticeable.
Example:

banana bənⓐnə

sibilant Sibilants are consonant sounds that make a hissing sound. This hiss comes from air rushing through a narrow valley along the speaker's tongue. A sibilant is a type of continuant.
Examples: /s/ (hiss), /z/ (buzz), /ʃ/ (mash)

soft palate This is the fleshy, flexible part at the back of the roof of the mouth. (same as *velum*)

stop sound A stop sound is made by stopping the airflow in the mouth so that the sound cannot continue. (compare *continuant sound*)
Examples: /t/ (sat), /d/ (sad), /p/ (cap)

stress The stressed syllable is the most important part of a word. It is mainly shown by lengthening the vowel and making it extra clear.
Examples:

Africa ⟨A⟩frica   Alaska Alⓐska

structure word Structure words – like pronouns, articles, and prepositions – do not carry as much information as content words, and they do not bring a picture to mind. They are usually not emphasized. (compare *content word*)
Examples: "the," "in," "will"

syllable A vowel itself, or a group of sounds with a vowel in the center. Syllables are the basic element of English rhythm.
Examples: Tom (1 syllable), a•tom (2 syllables), a•to•mic (3 syllables)

thought group A thought group is a group of words that belong together to make sense. They are often clauses or phrases or just short sentences. There is usually one focus word in each thought group.
Example: I want **tea** and a tuna **sand**wich.

velum (see *soft palate*)

vibration Vibration is the rapid, regular motion of the vocal cords that produces voicing.

vocal cords The vocal cords are a structure in the throat that can vibrate to produce a voicing noise. The vibration can be felt by placing your hand on your throat while making a voiced sound like /z/ or listening while closing your ears.

voiced sound Voiced sounds are made as the vocal cords vibrate. (compare *voiceless sounds*)
Examples: /v/ (lea**v**e), /z/ (buz**z**), /b/ (**b**at), /g/ (**g**oat)

voiceless sound Voiceless sounds are made without vibration of the vocal cords. (compare *voiced sound*)
Examples: /f/ (lea**f**), /s/ (bu**s**), /p/ (**p**at), /k/ (**c**oat)

vowel sound A vowel sound is made by not letting any part of the tongue touch any part of the inside of the mouth. A vowel sound is the most important part of a syllable. (compare *consonant sound*)
Examples: /iʸ/ (see), /eʸ/ (say), /oʷ/ (go)

weak syllable A syllable with a schwa /ə/ sound. It helps make the strong syllables easier to notice, by contrast.

whisper "Whisper" means to speak very quietly and without any voicing.

word group In *Clear Speech From the Start*, this term is used for a "thought group." (see *thought group*)

Bibliography

Acton, W. 2001. Integrated English speaking skills. In J. Murphy and P. Byrd (eds.), *Particular Approaches: Specialists' Perspectives on English Language Instruction*. Ann Arbor: University of Michigan Press. pp. 197–217.

Allen, V. 1971. Teaching intonation, from theory to practice. *TESOL Quarterly* 4 (1): 73–81.

Avery, P., and S. Ehrlich (eds.). 1992. *Teaching American English Pronunciation*. Oxford: Oxford University Press.

Bell, A. G. 1916. *The Mechanisms of Speech*. New York: Funk & Wagnalls.

Bolinger, D. 1986. *Intonation and Its Parts*. Stanford: Stanford University Press.

Bolinger, D. 1972. Accent is predictable (if you're a mind-reader). *Language* 48 (3): 633–644.

Bolinger, D. 1981. *Two Kinds of Vowels, Two Kinds of Rhythm*. Bloomington, IN: University of Indiana Linguistics Club.

Bradford, B. 1988. *Intonation in Context: Intonation Practice for Upper-Intermediate and Advanced Learners of English*. Cambridge: Cambridge University Press.

Brown, A. 1992. Twenty questions. In A. Brown (ed.), *Approaches to Pronunciation Teaching*. London: Macmillan, 1–17.

Brown, G. 1977, 1990. *Listening to Spoken English*. London: Longman.

Carney, E. 1994. *A Survey of English Spelling*. London, New York: Routledge.

Celce-Murcia, M., D. Brinton, and J. Goodwin. 1996, 2010. *Teaching Pronunciation: A Reference for Teachers of English to Speakers of Other Languages*. New York: Cambridge University Press.

Chun, D. 2002. *Discourse Intonation in L2: From Theory and Research to Practice*. Amsterdam: John Benjamins.

Dalton, C., and B. Seidlhofer. 1994. *Pronunciation*. Oxford: Oxford University Press.

David, D., L. Wade-Wooley, J. Kirby, and K. Smithrim. 2007. Reading and reading development in school-age children: A longitudinal study. *Journal of Research in Learning to Read* 30 (2): 169–183.

Derwing, T. M., and M. J. Rossiter. 2003. The effects of pronunciation instruction on the accuracy, fluency, and complexity of L2 accented speech. *Applied Language Learning* 13: 1–18.

Gilbert, J. B. 2012. *Clear Speech: Pronunciation and Listening Comprehension in North American English*, 4th ed. New York: Cambridge University Press.

Gilbert, J. B. 2001. Six pronunciation priorities for the beginning student. *The CATESOL Journal* 13 (1): 173–182.

Gilbert, J. B. 1999. Joseph Bogen: Clarifying the wine (implications of neurological research for language teaching). In D. Mendelsohn (ed.), *Expanding Our Vision: Insights for Language Teachers*. Oxford: Oxford University Press.

Gilbert, J. B. 1995. Pronunciation practice as an aid to listening comprehension. In D. Mendelsohn and J. Rubin (eds.), *A Guide for the Teaching of Second Language Listening*. San Diego: Dominie Press.

Gilbert, J. B. 2012. Myth: Intonation is hard to teach. In L. Grant (ed.), *Pronunciation Myths*. Ann Arbor: University of Michigan Press.

Gilbert, J. B. 1994. Intonation: A guide for the listener. In J. Morley (ed.), *Pronunciation Pedagogy and Theory*. TESOL:3–16.

Gilbert, J. B. 1987. Pronunciation and listening comprehension. In J. Morley (ed.), *Current Perspectives on Pronunciation: Practices Anchored in Theory*. TESOL: 29–40.

Goswami, U., and P. Bryant. 1990. *Phonological Skills and Learning to Read*. Hove: Psychology Press.

Grant, L. 2010. *Well Said: Pronunciation for Clear Communication*, 3rd ed. Boston: Heinle & Heinle.

Gumperz, J. J. 1982. *Discourse Strategies*. Cambridge: Cambridge University Press.

Hahn, L. 2004. Primary stress and intelligibility: Research to motivate the teaching of suprasegmentals. *TESOL Quarterly* 30 (2): 201–223.

Hirst, D., and A. Di Cristo. 1998. *Intonation Systems: A Survey of Twenty Languages*. Cambridge: Cambridge University Press.

Kjellin, O. 1999. Accent addition: Prosody and perception facilitate second language learning. In O. Fujimura, B. D. Joseph, and B. Paled (eds.), *Proceedings of Linguistics and Phonetics Conference 1998*. The Karolinum Press, Prague. 2: 373–398.

McNerny, M., and D. Mendelsohn. 1992. Suprasegmentals in the pronunciation class: Setting priorities. In P. Avery and S. Ehrlich (eds.), *Teaching American English Pronunciation*. Oxford: Oxford University Press.

Miller, S. 2000. *Targeting Pronunciation*. Boston: Houghton-Mifflin.

Morley, J. 1992. *Rapid Review of Vowel & Prosodic Contexts*. Ann Arbor: University of Michigan Press.

Munro, M., and T. Derwing. 2011. The foundations of accent and intelligibility in pronunciation research, *Language Teaching.* Cambridge University Press, 44 (3), 316–327.

Wade-Wooley, L., and C. Wood. 2006. Prosodic sensitivity and reading development. *Journal of Research in Reading* 29: 253–257.

Wennerstrom, A. 1991. *The Music of Everyday Speech: Prosody and Discourse Analysis.* Oxford: Oxford University Press.

Notes